HAPHAZARD BY STARLIGHT

A poem a day from Advent to Epiphany

Janet Morley

First published in Great Britain in 2013

Society for Promoting Christian Knowledge
36 Causton Street
London SW1P 4ST
www.spckpublishing.co.uk

Copyright acknowledgements can be found on pp. 143–5.

British Library Cataloguing-in-Publication Data
A catalogue record for this book is available from the British Library

ISBN 978–0–281–07062–6

Typeset by Caroline Waldron, Wirral, Cheshire
Printed in Great Britain by Ashford Colour Press
Subsequently digitally printed in Great Britain

Produced on paper from sustainable forests

Contents

Contents

Contents

Contents

Introduction

———•◦•———

Almighty God,
give us grace that we may cast away the works of darkness
and put upon us the armour of light,
now in the time of this mortal life,
in which thy Son Jesus Christ came to visit us in great humility;
that in the last day
when he shall come again in his glorious majesty
to judge both the quick and the dead,
we may rise to the life immortal;
through him who liveth and reigneth with thee and the Holy Spirit,
now and for ever.

Collect for Advent Sunday (BCP 1662)

The themes of the season

Advent, like Lent, is a time of waiting. It is a preparation time for Christmas and the mystery of the Incarnation, just as Lent prepares for Holy Week and the mystery of the resurrection at Easter. In both periods, Christians have traditionally practised prayer, fasting and self-examination, and reflected on some quite penitential themes before the period of feasting and celebration. It is worth seeking to spend time with the themes that belong with Advent. They are not all comfortable, but can provide a welcome and realistic contrast with the glitzy and occasionally exhausting merriment of the commercial Christmas that is sold to us. And the period can thereby lead us into a deeper and more grounded sense of joy and mystery.

The collect for Advent Sunday sets a tone that is both expectant and somewhat fearful. It looks forward to the nativity, when Jesus Christ 'came to visit us in great humility'. The phrase recalls the ancient Christian poem in Philippians 2 in which God's self-emptying love in becoming human is proclaimed, and it recalls the Old Testament God who 'visits' or pitches his tent among us. But the expectation is surrounded with images of struggle, mortality and judgement. To recall the child at Bethlehem is also to recall the end time when Christ will 'come again in his glorious majesty' to hold to account the living and the dead. And a profound battle is announced between the works and forces of darkness and the light that is to come; there is a sense that we must engage with death in order to understand the nature of eternal life.

In the northern hemisphere it is significant that the period of Advent coincides with the time of year when the days are becoming ever shorter and darkness predominates as we come towards the solstice. Often the weather is extremely cold, or at least filthy and unpredictable, and travel may be difficult or even dangerous. Winter illnesses are on the increase and death is more common in the elderly. Poverty becomes harder to endure as fuel is both necessary and costly. Whereas in Lent the spring is gradually making itself felt, in Advent plants, trees and wildlife are retreating into their winter dormancy, in the effort to survive the time of greatest austerity. And then, it is no coincidence that we have chosen to celebrate the birth of the saviour, the coming of light into the world, at the time of year when for countless generations humans have celebrated the return of the sun, announcing the turn of the year and the expectation of growing daylight and warmth.

As well as considering apocalyptic themes, it is a time to reflect on some of the key people at the heart of the traditional stories – those on earth who were willing to cooperate with heaven for the sake of our salvation. Central among these is Mary, and the story of the annunciation and her willingness to accept rejection and danger in order to bear the holy child takes centre stage. It is interesting to see how many poets have focused on the encounter between Mary and the angel, the poignant human experience at the heart of it, and the parallels that can be drawn with 'annunciations' that we too may experience.

The event at the centre of Christmas – the birth of an infant in humble circumstances – is full of an intimate sort of awe, but it also reminds us of the precarious conditions of our mortality. As anyone who has ever given birth can testify, this joyful occasion is only achieved through fear and pain, and a heightened sense of the dangers that surround our fragile human life. The nativity story conveys not just glory and hope, but threat and suffering, political danger and the need to take flight. The slaughter of the children by Herod follows hard after Christmas Day, and the period includes the feast of Christianity's first martyr, the deacon Stephen. Traditionally, carols that rejoice in the birth of the infant Christ also see the shadow of his death foretold – the cradle and the cross are reflected in each other. As we move to the feast day of the Epiphany, the Church celebrates how the whole drama of salvation was shown forth to the Gentiles, represented by the foreign seekers known as the magi or the kings.

A number of Christian poets have consciously drawn on this mixture of themes, or highlighted some paradoxical elements, linking the Christian narrative with our own lives in time. Others without a religious intent have nevertheless explored themes that are suggested by the Advent period, or engage with winter and the turning of the year in ways that concur with Christian meditation in this season.

There was a poem made

In the days of Caesar, when his subjects went to be reckoned,
there was a poem made, too dark for him (naive with power) to
    read.
It was a bunch of shepherds who discovered
in Bethlehem of Judah, the great music beyond reason and
    reckoning.

Waldo Williams, translated from the Welsh by Rowan Williams

Why is poetry a particularly suitable literary form for meditating on the mystery of the Incarnation? In the poem chosen for Christmas Eve, the Welsh poet Waldo Williams uses a bold metaphor to convey this mystery. He speaks of it as a poem made by God in the world, noticed by 'a bunch of shepherds' but 'too dark' for the powers that be to comprehend. The image uses the fact that poetry is allusive and subtle, even when it is on the surface deceptively simple or even conversational. Poetry yields its multi-layered meanings only when the reader pays attention, and spends time reflecting on what may be a very few words. Intuition and a certain humility are needed, along with a willingness to notice properly the detailed world that the poem illuminates, and perhaps to be personally transformed by the resulting insights. As readers we have to bring some deep parts of ourselves into the process of interpretation; we have to surrender to the poem. At the same time, a poem doesn't browbeat the reader: it intrigues, challenges and delights.

Nothing could be further from the method of poetry than the plain-spoken 'executive summaries' that are commonly the only sort of document the powerful players in our world have time to consult. But it is very like the method God seems to choose in relating to humankind. Like the Incarnation, poetry is located in the 'scandal of particularity' and draws its power from this. It is similarly appreciated most readily by those who themselves are not too busy or important to attend to the details of what is going on. People are not usually moved or touched by generalizations, but by concrete image, story, presence. The eternal is best captured for contemplation in a 'grain of sand' (Blake), or in a tiny baby. So there is a sense in which the making of a poem reflects the action of the Word of God who was made particular flesh in our world at Christmas. The poetic approach goes deep into the way we are made, as well as the way God typically is able to be heard by us. As Rowan Williams put it in his 2012 lecture to the Waldo Williams Society: 'The enterprise of poetry is taking us to the level of primordial language, primitive language; ultimately, the word of God – the speech which underlies our humanity, indeed our very being.'

Poetry is a powerful image for what we ourselves may become in the hands of God, as we respond to his love in Christ. Waldo Williams' poem ends with the stunning image of God as poet, not only fashioning the great 'music beyond reason and reckoning' of the Incarnation, but also remaking us into beautiful and telling poetry ourselves. It is as if God needs our responsive hearts in order to compose the great hymn of praise, inhabited by the whole creation: 'He seeks us out as wordhoard for his workmanship, the laureate of heaven.'

This book is an attempt to join in with this divine, creative impulse.

How to use this book

Haphazard by Starlight is written with the individual reader in mind, taking a daily path through the Advent and Christmas period, up to Epiphany. It can obviously be read as it is laid out day by day. But it is important to remember that there exists no 'canon' or agreed 'lectionary' of suitable poems to reflect on during this time of year. The chosen sequence is intuitive (and when I compared it with a friend's independent selection of poetry for exactly the same devotional exercise, we found only one overlap in our choices). So you may prefer sometimes to find your own poems that work for you in this season; or perhaps my choices will introduce you to poets whose work you are prompted to explore further. My commentaries are my own readings of the poems, but every reader will find more to say, and will sometimes disagree with points made by me.

The book could also be used in a group meeting during Advent, but very few groups would be likely to convene during the Christmas period itself. Perhaps an Epiphany meeting could look back over the poems chosen around Christmas. Inevitably, readers would need to use the material in a devotional way individually first, and compare notes. But precisely because poems benefit greatly from being read aloud, and because one person on their own will seldom mine all the treasure of meaning in a text, there is a lot to be said for creating a reading group to get the most out of *Haphazard by Starlight*. Here are some suggested ways of grouping poems and comparing them (there are many others):

- **Autumn** (Advent Calendar; November Sonnet; Autumn's Fall; Shadows)
- **Searching** (The Other; The Absence; Church Going)
- **Fear** (Dover Beach; Ozymandias; The Second Coming; The Tyger)

- **Darkness and light** (We grow accustomed to the Dark; Darkness; Blackbird in Fulham)
- **Annunciation** (Black Rook in Rainy Weather; The Bat; Annunciation; The Annunciation; The Visitation; Northumbrian Sequence, 4)
- **Winter celebration** (At the Winter Solstice; Ode to Winter; seasonal *ghazal*)
- **Nativity** (In the Days of Caesar; BC:AD; A Christmas Carol; Christmas)
- **Birth, suffering and death** (Innocent's Song; Song for a Winter Birth; Musée des Beaux Arts; The Year's Midnight; Journey of the Magi)
- **Vulnerability and care** (Agnus Dei; Woman to Child)
- **Hope** ('Ring out, wild bells'; Winter Paradise; God's Grandeur)

1 December

Advent Calendar

He will come like last leaf's fall.
One night when the November wind
has flayed the trees to bone, and earth
wakes choking on the mould,
the soft shroud's folding.

He will come like frost.
One morning when the shrinking earth
opens on mist, to find itself
arrested in the net
of alien, sword-set beauty.

He will come like dark.
One evening when the bursting red
December sun draws up the sheet
and penny-masks its eye to yield
the star-snowed fields of sky.

He will come, will come,
will come like crying in the night,
like blood, like breaking,
as the earth writhes to toss him free.
He will come like child.

Rowan Williams

The poem is called 'Advent Calendar' – the traditional way to mark the progress of December towards Christmas Day – and it shows the movement of time through its length. Starting at the end of

November, it is clearly deep December by the third stanza. The landscape and the weather become progressively colder, darker and more wintry, as the poem charts the very end of autumn, with its mounds of choking leaf mould, moving to hard frosts, early sunsets, deep darkness and the expectation of snow. Throughout this sequence, there is the insistently repeated phrase – almost a cry – 'He will come'. It is a kind of promise, like a response to the ancient Christian liturgical call 'Maranatha – come, Lord Jesus!', or the hymn 'O come, O come Emmanuel'. But the chilling images of *how* he will come make the promise sound fearful rather than reassuring.

'Like last leaf's fall' – this is the silent and unnoticed moment when autumn passes finally into winter and the deciduous trees no longer retain any sign of their summer life. Their trunks and branches are fully exposed and bare, but the poet intensifies the image by using the language of torture to describe how the wind has 'flayed the trees to bone'. The idea of the trees having 'bones' starts to depict the landscape itself as instinct with human life, something that is reiterated in the image of the earth waking, choked with leaves. The imagery of 'choking on the mould', and 'the soft shroud', following the language of flaying, reiterate the sinister and life-threatening atmosphere of this wintry scene. The deceptively gentle words like 'soft' and 'folding' are applied not to a blanket of leaves, but to a shroud for a corpse. At this stage there is no explicit mention of the human community who have to navigate the world during the ravages of winter; instead, human reactions have been imputed to the natural world. Human struggles are suggested without needing to be mentioned, but we have a growing sense of the created world being itself identified with human violence, suffering, and the need for redemption.

The second stanza does nothing to dispel this impression. Here, the hard frost surprises a wakening earth which shrinks to find itself 'arrested'. The choice of words brilliantly conveys the actual qualities of frost: leaf litter does actually shrink and curl, and then set hard and motionless – arrested – as the moisture content within it is frozen. But the language is that of fear and of being brutally awoken by a dawn raid, to be taken into custody. There is a kind of beauty, as there is with deep frost, but it is frightening, like a strange kind of imprisonment. The landscape is caught 'in the net/ of alien, sword-set beauty'. There are nets, and swords – we are in the arena of life and death combat.

The third stanza, about the promise of the dark, is a bit more playful, though even here the atmosphere is odd and sinister. It describes a wintry sunset, where the ball of the sun looks red and huge as it slides towards the horizon. But the size of the sun is indicated by the word 'bursting' – again there is the feeling that something terrifying, like an explosion, could be about to happen. The swift sunset is conveyed by suggesting that the sun is drawing up the earth over its face like a mask, like a child playing peep-bo with a bed sheet. Or it could suggest the way one draws a sheet over the face of someone who has just died. The stanza ends with some more cold beauty – the 'star-snowed fields of sky'. Again there is repeated transfer of meanings, intensifying the sense of strangeness, as the stars are compared to thick snowflakes and the sky itself has 'fields'. The effect is to suggest snow when it is not yet snowing (but it will), and that the fields beneath the sky are caught up with it as the kingdom of the dark becomes complete.

So we reach the final stanza, which initially refuses to reveal the image, which we are now expecting, of how 'he will come'. But then there is a terrible list. It will be fearful: 'like crying in the night', 'like blood', 'like breaking'. The image is of the earth 'writhing' with pain. The previous verses have led us to anticipate the worst, and yet it suddenly becomes apparent that this is not combat, or arrest, or torture, or imprisonment; it is childbirth. This, of course, typically involves crying, and blood, and breaking, and writhing – 'he will come like child'. The omission of the article somehow emphasizes the routine ordinariness of how babies are born. But strangely, it is shockingly unexpected when we think about the coming of the Christchild.

The mood of this poem could hardly be further from the sentimentality that is commonly found in our Christmas celebrations. But the tone is absolutely traditional for Advent. The Christchild will come, but not until the world is at its darkest, and there will be struggle and violence surrounding the event. The preparation involves a stripping down, a facing of fear, and an acceptance of the dark. It will be both utterly ordinary and yet apocalyptic. There is a sense of the second coming of Christ implicit in our forthcoming celebration of the first coming. And the earth itself wrestles with us to greet redemption. In the words of St Paul, 'the whole creation has been groaning together in travail until now' (Romans 8.22). Only through the pain of a crucial childbirth will the agonies of human conflict and violence be addressed.

As we enter the season of Advent, what is the balance in your heart between hope and fear?

INFHAZARD BY JANET HOPLEY
STARLIGHT

Rowan Williams

December

7¹⁄₂   primordal language

2   "he will come"

1   " the stars — "nowed folds of sky"

2 December

---·◆·---

November Sonnet

Spirit of place. Spirit of time. Re-form
The rugged oaks and chestnuts. Now they stand
Naked and pallid giants out of storm
And out of sorts. It is the Autumn's end

And this is Winter brought in by All Saints
Fast followed by All Souls to keep us in
Touch with chill and death. Each re-acquaints
Us with the year's end. Yet we now begin

A life of realism, watching out
For a red sunset, grateful for a dawn
Of rich light now. Tall shadows step and strut

Facing the big wind daily coming on
Faster. This is the season of right doubt
While that elected child waits to be born.

Elizabeth Jennings

Like the previous poem by Rowan Williams, this one is set on the cusp
of autumn's end as it moves into winter. It is constructed as a trad-
itional sonnet: the first eight lines propose the theme, and then there
is a subtle turn into the last six lines, which offer some interpretation
of the theme. The poet mostly uses the formal conventions of the
sonnet, but also varies them. She creates unexpected gaps between
lines, disrupting their expected rhythm and line endings, and eventu-
ally loosening the severe rhyme scheme of the first half, rather as the
November wind in the poem reshapes and unsettles the trees.

It starts in a very abrupt way, with short phrases that are not real sentences. It isn't clear whether the poet is addressing the spirits of place and time, and briskly instructing them to re-form the major trees in the landscape, or is describing what the movement of the seasons is actually doing to a location in violent gusts of wind that stop and start. There is a sense that the stripping of the trees causes a kind of indecent violation of the dignity of 'rugged oaks and chestnuts', leaving them uncomfortably exposed and uncertain; they are acknowledged giants of the landscape, but are now left 'naked and pallid'. It is not quite like the violent 'flaying' of Williams' poem, but the trees are 'out of storm/ And out of sorts'. There is a clever juxtaposition of phrases starting 'out of', where the first describes the event that caused the change of status, and the second is a metaphor for feeling disconcerted or as if things are not right. Again, human reactions are imputed to trees and their fate; but the reader is implicitly invited to identify with them as winter approaches.

The poet now announces the end of autumn and the arrival of winter, linking these to the Church's liturgical pattern that has been developing during the month just gone. All Saints and All Souls (1 and 2 November), which commemorate both the heroes of the Christian tradition and our personally beloved dead, immediately follow the autumn festival of Hallowe'en (itself overlaying the pagan traditions of Samhain), when the dead are supposed to walk. November is known as the time of remembrance, when the living are invited to come close to those who have died. Inevitably and appropriately these festivals are about keeping us 'in/ Touch with chill and death' and our own expectations of mortality. But notice how the poem divides 'in' and 'Touch' by the placing of the line ending. The connection between the living and the dead may be there, but it is disjointed.

By the end of the first eight lines – the octet – the poem has announced its sense of the inescapability of remembering and experiencing once again the year's end. It is a chilly and unsettling prospect; but then there is a change of tone, which happens on the hinge of the poem, between the octave and the sestet (the last six lines). It is as if the reader is led into a sense of acceptance that embraces the positive elements of the year's death. Although we usually think of this as being at the end of December (or possibly on the solstice on the 21st), Jennings has clearly invoked the Church's own liturgical calendar, and this begins afresh at the beginning of Advent. After the month that is about remembering the dead, what we move into is 'a life of realism', which enables a sense of gratitude for the light that remains, which can have its own beauty and richness, scarce as it is.

Again the poem strains against the line ending as it moves into the final three lines, but there is a sense of increasing strength as it does so. It appears that the trees that were initially shamed and discomfited by their forcible stripping have now found a confidence and power. They 'step and strut' and face into the 'big wind' boldly, even though it is coming on faster. Without the ballast of their leaves, they are not actually in such danger from the storms as they were in autumn; of course, the implication is that for human beings it is similar. To submit to a time of stripping down and austerity will leave us stronger in the end.

The announcement that 'this is the season of right doubt' is rather heartening and intriguing. It suggests that there is a deep rightness in accepting the darkness of doubt and uncertainty on our spiritual journey, reflected as it is in the seasonal growing of the dark and the cold. There is an appropriate place for letting ourselves go into what is unknown and unsure. It may well be not just a good way but the only way to prepare for the mystery that will appear. Only in the last line do we receive the reassurance that the 'elected child waits to be born'.

'This is the season of right doubt'. When in your life have you experienced doubt as something that seemed 'right'?

3 December

Autumn's Fall

It seems the rain will be its end – the smell
of rotting-down in ditches, under trees,
the sharp scent of late apples in wet grass,
the spent leaves guttering in the stone-flagged well.

The spaces in the branches stretch and grow.
High spiralling of crows in the thin sky.
The grey drift of the distance. Nothing more
of hope or exultation in the flow

of damp air from the windows that I leave
to let the year move quietly through the house
preparing for the long dark and the cold,
loosening the nets spent thoughts still weave,

clingy as cobwebs. There must be space for death,
and witness for this seep of emptying light;
for winter, pressing with the cattle at the gate,
clouding the darkness with their frightened breath.

Kerry Hardie

This poem about the end of autumn has another tone again, com-
pared with 'Advent Calendar' and 'November Sonnet'. It is conversa-
tional and low key, beginning as if the theme of the poem has already
been stated and there is no need to explain what is being referred to.
There are no abrupt or even confident announcements; the poem
meanders quietly through the four verses with a feeling of attenu-
ation and letting go, rather than active struggle. It is as if the year end

comes uncertainly and with a gradual decline – not with blustering storms or a dramatic stripping, either of trees or human hearts.

The first stanza begins tentatively – 'It seems the rain will be its end'. The movement from autumn to winter is noticed as having already occurred through the outdoor scents rather than the sight of the landscape. We become aware of the compost smell of ditches choked with died-back vegetation, and of the conclusion of the period of fruitfulness through the sharp tang of useless late windfall apples that are now rotting in the sodden grass. The well is clogged with 'spent leaves' – the language suggests exhaustion, and the word 'guttering' manages to imply both the filthy and sluggish state that rainwater gutters get into after massive leaf fall and a dying of the light (since it is usually candles that gutter as they reach the end of their useful life).

The second stanza does include, if not exactly hope or exhilaration, a certain sort of looking up, as the winter sky becomes more visible. Instead of commenting on the trees themselves, the poem notices the 'spaces in the branches'; it is the sky and the gaps between things that grow and stretch. Yet the sky itself is 'thin', and the 'high spiralling of crows' creates a sense of the distantness of any activity (which itself is just circling rather than going anywhere). This sense of directionless, languid wafting movement is emphasized by an abstract 'grey drift of distance', and by the way the poet increasingly omits proper verbs.

As we reach the mid-point of the poem it is explicitly stated that hope and exultation are exhausted – yet the poet takes the sentence on into the next stanza, so that 'the flow/ of damp air' seems to move lazily between the verses. It seems that we have been inside the head of someone who is watching the gradual dissolution of the landscape from her home. It is hard to detect quite whether the damp air is flowing into the open windows or out from them – perhaps the movement both ways is intended. The narrator speaks of letting not just the air but 'the year' move quietly through the house. (The word 'open' is not used, but the reader supplies it; in the same way we need to respond with openness to the dissolution that winter brings.) Somehow the action of airing the rooms, perhaps cleaning away cobwebs and brushing curtains, before sealing up draughts for the winter, is turning into an acceptance of a period of clearing the heart and the mind for enduring a time of darkness or loss. It is time to move on from, or step back from, the activities and expectations of the summer, which are now irrelevant. The 'spent thoughts' that hang around echo the 'spent leaves' of the first stanza that were clogging the water source. If you speak out loud the line 'loosening the nets spent thoughts still weave', you will hear what a tongue-twister it is – as if caught in a net.

The fourth stanza starts still draped with the thoughts that are 'clingy as cobwebs'. But then there is the strongest statement made in the poem: 'there must be space for death'. This could have several meanings: that grief following bereavement requires its proper time to be worked through; that the dying back in winter is a natural part of a seasonal cycle and takes its own time, or that we humans should consciously try to let go of what needs to die, and that space and solitude may be necessary in order to achieve this. There is also the need for a 'witness' to the dying process the poem has been charting. Perhaps the other seasons have more obvious glories, and many poetic advocates to extol them. This poem mentions just 'this seep of emptying light'; it is hardly possible to be enthusiastic about universal shutting down, and yet the poem convinces the reader that it is necessary and must be surrendered to.

The poem ends on quite a fearful note. The light is fading, and there is a sense that winter, without having announced itself in a definite way up until this point, is now a weighty presence, 'pressing with the cattle at the gate'. This arresting image captures the observation of chilly cows huddling at one end of a field to take what advantage they can of the diminishing shelter offered by the hedges, and perhaps looking to receive winter fodder, as the grass dies back. The final line merges the breath of the cattle (rhyming with 'death'), now visible because of the cold, with the early darkness. And their breath is described as 'frightened'. This is a brilliant double shift. If anything, it is the cattle themselves that may be nervous, not their breath (the part to suggest the whole). But more likely, the image compels because it is an acute portrayal of our own human fear, which we project onto the natural world when we are surrounded with a darkness that is growing ever murkier.

As we enter the season of dying back and stripping down, is there anything about your own life that is 'clingy as cobwebs' and needs to be let go of?

4 December

Shadows

And if tonight my soul may find her peace
in sleep, and sink in good oblivion,
and in the morning wake like a new-opened flower
then I have been dipped again in God, and new-created.

And if, as weeks go round, in the dark of the moon
my spirit darkens and goes out, and soft, strange gloom
pervades my movements and my thoughts and words
then I shall know that I am walking still
with God, we are close together now the moon's in shadow.

And if, as autumn deepens and darkens
I feel the pain of falling leaves, and stems that break in storms
and trouble and dissolution and distress
and then the softness of deep shadows folding, folding
around my soul and spirit, around my lips
so sweet, like a swoon, or more like the drowse of a low, sad song
singing darker than the nightingale, on, on to the solstice
and the silence of short days, the silence of the year, the shadow,
then I shall know that my life is moving still
with the dark earth, and drenched
with the deep oblivion of earth's lapse and renewal.

And if, in the changing phases of man's life
I fall in sickness and in misery
my wrists seem broken and my heart seems dead
and strength is gone, and my life
is only the leavings of a life:

and still, among it all, snatches of lovely oblivion, and snatches of
 renewal
odd, wintry flowers upon the withered stem, yet new, strange
 flowers
such as my life has not brought forth before, new blossoms of me –

then I must know that still
I am in the hands [of] the unknown God,
he is breaking me down to his own oblivion
to send me forth on a new morning, a new man.

D. H. Lawrence

This poem by Lawrence embraces the shadows of the falling light
of autumn, and it does so from the start. The peaceful mood of the
first line, the conviction that oblivion can be 'good', and the sense
of being in the hands of God are both the starting point and the
repeated conclusion of the poem, returned to again and again in the
interim stanzas. The whole poem, with its free rhythms, is a kind
of spiral that is perhaps intended to mirror the productive cycle of
the seasons, in which dying and dissolution have their strangely
comforting place. Different kinds of 'oblivion' are encountered. The
first stanza is about sleeping and yet waking refreshed. The second
speaks of the growing darkness of the season, with its consequent
low moods – and yet these can be accepted as part of a cycle like
the monthly dark of the moon. The third and fourth stanzas take
us on towards the solstice of life, with the sense that one's powers
are beginning to fail in age. Yet all can be seen as part of a natural
process in which one is held and nurtured by God.

It is almost like an incantation, as it flows smoothly on. The phrase
'and if' recurs again and again, followed by some exploration of how
the soul or the spirit or the emotions, or the health of the narrator
may be weakened, just as the seasons ebb and flow and the moon
waxes and wanes. Each time there is a reassuring answering phrase
starting with 'then': 'then I have been dipped again in God'; 'then
I shall know that I am walking still/ with God . . . that my life is
moving still/ with the dark earth . . . that still/ I am in the hands [of]
the unknown God'. There are other repetitions, including the word

'oblivion': 'sink in good oblivion', 'deep oblivion of the earth's lapse and renewal', 'snatches of lovely oblivion', 'breaking me down to his own oblivion'.

Like the preceding poems in this book, the narrator mingles his human feelings, thoughts and experience with natural cycles and phenomena. He speaks of his spirit darkening with the dark of the moon as it wanes; of feeling the 'pain of falling leaves, and stems that break in storms', of being enfolded in 'the softness of deep shadows' as the year moves towards the solstice, of feeling his life 'drenched' in the earth's autumnal dieback. Notice how immensely long the sentence is that makes up the third stanza. It is 11 lines long, the list of troubles merging into the surrounding shadows, and the shadows then repeatedly folding back on themselves. The poem uses words with hard staccato consonants for the troubles: 'stems', 'storms', 'trouble', 'dissolution', 'distress'; but then suggests a gentle enfolding of these through repeated use of the soft letter 'w': 'shadows', 'sweet', 'swoon', 'drowse', 'low'.

The next stanza expresses matters much more plainly and starkly. Here we have a sense of a person facing deep old age, with real loss of strength highlighted in a crucial part of the body ('my wrists seem broken'), and lack of motivation expressed in the seemingly 'dead' heart and the sense that what remains is only rubbish. Yet the next stanza answers even this stage of life. The oblivion is still referred to as 'lovely', and the narrator holds out the possibility that there may yet emerge strange new 'snatches of renewal'. Again he uses floral images, envisaging 'odd, wintry flowers upon the withered stem', which may even be 'new blossoms of me'.

The last stanza sums up what seems to be a deeply encouraging act of faith in the 'unknown God' who breaks us down like leaf mould and then remakes us and brings forth new flowers. It is very soothing and restful, compared with the much more astringent poems about autumn and human letting go that precede it here. Lawrence's landscape is consistently gentle; the weather does not come over as cold, or smelly, or frightening, or at all uncomfortable to be 'drenched' in. And yet there may be a good deal of recognition for the reader in the human experiences that these natural metaphors stand for: ageing, failure, loss of strength, illness, the sense of having left to one 'only the leavings of a life'. And there is a real courage about accepting that, as part of the natural world ourselves, we move towards inevitable bodily oblivion; but we may face this prospect with equanimity, since we are held in it always by God.

Are there some genuine losses in your life (including loss of your own powers) that you need to accept and embrace? To what extent are you able to feel held in God's hands?

5 December

―――――•―•――•―――

Black Rook in Rainy Weather

On the stiff twig up there
Hunches a wet black rook
Arranging and rearranging its feathers in the rain.
I do not expect a miracle
Or an accident

To set the sight on fire
In my eye, nor seek
Any more in the desultory weather some design,
But let spotted leaves fall as they fall,
Without ceremony, or portent.

Although, I admit, I desire,
Occasionally, some backtalk
From the mute sky, I can't honestly complain:
A certain minor light may still
Lean incandescent

Out of kitchen table or chair
As if a celestial burning took
Possession of the most obtuse objects now and then –
Thus hallowing an interval
Otherwise inconsequent

By bestowing largesse, honor,
One might say love. At any rate, I now walk
Wary (for it could happen
Even in this dull, ruinous landscape); skeptical,
Yet politic; ignorant

5 December

Of whatever angel may choose to flare
Suddenly at my elbow. I only know that a rook
Ordering its black feathers can so shine
As to seize my senses, haul
My eyelids up, and grant

A brief respite from fear
Of total neutrality. With luck,
Trekking stubborn through this season
Of fatigue, I shall
Patch together a content

Of sorts. Miracles occur,
If you care to call those spasmodic
Tricks of radiance miracles. The wait's begun again,
The long wait for the angel,
For that rare, random descent.

Sylvia Plath

Plath's poem could hardly be more different in mood from Lawrence's, although both of them could be said to represent explorations into the mysterious source of poetic inspiration. This one has a deliberately unsensational, indeed rather humdrum title, something that is mirrored in the flat, matter-of-fact language that dominates much of the poem. It is the opposite of hypnotic. The lines are not of a regular length or rhythm, and at first glance the poem seems rather free and unstructured, with the narrator's thoughts just going along in an associative way.

On closer inspection, however, we notice that it is very carefully constructed indeed, both in the ideas that are juxtaposed and in the choosing and placing of words and whole lines. Each of the eight stanzas has five lines. Although they do not have a regular 'beat', the middle line is usually longer than the others, and the last word in each line is a half-rhyme with the line in that position in every other stanza: 'there', 'fire', 'desire', 'chair', and so forth. These soft half-rhymes are subtle and nowhere near as noticeable as a full rhyme, but they have a cumulative impact.

The poem sets forth in an apparently conversational fashion, pointing out an ordinary bird preening its ordinary black feathers on a gloomy wet day. Yet by the fourth line we are alerted that something quite extraordinary is being awaited: 'I do not expect a miracle'. The narrator, who is presented as heavy-handedly sceptical and down to earth throughout (or at least trying to be), succeeds in introducing through denial an idea about transcendence that was hardly about to occur to the reader, who is still just noticing a well-observed perfectly natural creature. ('Hunches' is a completely accurate word for the shape of a big bird who is disconsolate about its wet feathers.) What miracle is that? As if apologizing for the introduction of such a dramatic word, the term 'accident' is immediately offered as an alternative.

The sentence is left hanging as we proceed to the next stanza and discover the narrator's longing – so at odds with her prosaic demeanour – that she might experience having her sight 'set on fire' as she walks through the woods. We are reminded of various poets (such as Emily Dickinson) who attest to a special kind of seeing that is sometimes available to them, and is deeply precious. But also there may be an echo of biblical moments of suddenly seeing the world differently by the grace of God (for example, 2 Kings 6.17; Luke 24.31). The narrator hastens to emphasize the completely unmiraculous nature of the 'desultory weather' and the ugly 'spotted leaves' that fall in autumn. Again, she denies looking for any portentous meaning in them.

But the third stanza then backtracks from the assertion, admitting to a wish for 'backtalk' from the 'mute sky'. Remarkable as such a thing might be, the choice of a colloquial word like 'backtalk' makes it sound not unreasonable. This tone is maintained as she confesses, 'I can't honestly complain' (as if a more querulous person might feel entitled to do so when the sky refuses to speak). And then she proceeds to describe experiences of seeing mundane objects take on an extraordinary light that touches them with transcendence. The poem conveys this odd sort of moment by mingling language that is downbeat and understated ('a certain minor light', 'the most obtuse objects', 'inconsequent') with the outright mystical ('lean incandescent', 'celestial burning', 'took possession', 'bestowing largesse').

Perhaps the 'obtuse' objects stand for the narrator herself when she feels stubbornly lacking in inspiration.

In the fourth stanza, the narrator finally arrives at what the gift might be, but puts it tentatively: 'one might say love'. And then she immediately disowns such ecstasy, with a disparaging 'At any rate', stressing her scepticism (and yet it could happen, the bracketed lines yearningly point out, even in this unpromising landscape). Again, on the hinge of the last line of the verse we are suddenly catapulted into the possibility of an angel choosing to 'flare' at her elbow. The choice of the word 'flare' is exact, suggesting a suddenly ignited flame that makes you flinch and turn away for self-protection. She is both expecting an angel and expecting to be taken by surprise by any such appearance.

Then comes the assertion that lies at the heart of the poem and perhaps at what is understood to be the core of poetic inspiration: 'I only know that a rook/ Ordering its black feathers can so shine/ As to seize my senses, haul/ My eyelids up ...' The intense observation of the world in all its ordinariness and 'thisness' is the locus where a vision of glory is granted. The language is quite rough – 'seize', 'haul' – as if the poet has to be grabbed by the world and shaken to make her see in this special way.

In a way that has become familiar, the narrative style instantly deflates again (so fleeting is the experience) and is back in the half-depressed world of the fear of neutrality, of the need to trudge through 'this season/ Of fatigue' and make the best of things, to 'Patch together a content/ Of sorts'. There is one final combination of assertion and denial: miracles occur – or are they just 'tricks of radiance'? Then comes the admission the narrator has been painfully working round to throughout the poem: that she is waiting for an angel, 'that rare, random descent'. In describing the exhausting –and for a modern, sceptical woman, embarrassing – wait for a kind of annunciation, she has constructed a stunning poem that is precisely about that.

What do you understand to be the source of your own inspiration or creativity? Are you open to experiencing the 'descent of an angel'?

6 December

The Other

Whatever I find if I search will be wrong.
I must wait: sternest trial of all, to sit
Passive, receptive, and patient, empty
Of every demand and desire, until
That other, that being I never would have found
Though I spent my whole life in the quest, will step
From the shadows, approach like a wild, awkward child.

And this will be the longest task: to attend,
To open myself. To still my energy
Is harder than to use it in any cause.
Yet surely she will only be revealed
By pushing against the grain of my nature
That always yearns for choice. I feel it painful
And strong as a birth in which there is no pause.

I must hold myself back from every lure of action
To let her come closer, a wary smile on her face,
One arm lifted – to greet me or ward off attack
(I cannot decipher that uncertain gesture).
I must even control the pace of my breath
Until she has drawn her circle near enough
To capture the note of her faint reedy voice.

And then as in dreams, when a language unspoken
Since times before childhood is recalled
(When I was as timid as she, my forgotten sister –
Her presence my completion and reward),

I begin to understand, in fragments, the message
She waited so long to deliver. Loving her I shall learn
My own secret at last from the words of her song.

Ruth Fainlight

This poem explores the crucial importance of waiting within the spiritual life. This is a strange notion within our contemporary culture, where advice to anyone seeking a more fulfilling life commonly takes the approach of taking active responsibility for making something happen. In Sylvia Plath's poem we have seen the struggle of the narrator to wait on the arrival of an 'angel' to transform her way of viewing the world (and indeed the struggle to believe/disbelieve that such a thing is possible). Here, the one who is awaited is described initially simply as 'the other'. Quite who is being referred to is one of the intriguing aspects of the poem.

There are some interesting paradoxes in the Christian tradition of searching for, or waiting upon, the presence of God. There are sayings of Jesus that seem to proclaim that it is a straightforward matter of asking in faith ('Ask, and it will be given you; seek, and you will find; knock, and it will be opened to you' – Matthew 7.7). However, there is also a very strong biblical witness to the passionate search that has not yet been fulfilled, for instance in many of the Psalms and in particular the Song of Songs (see 5.6). These passages have been of great importance to contemplative religious through the ages, no doubt because generations of Christian followers have discovered that asking in faith is not as simple as it sounds – or else that achieving the necessary simplicity is hard. The effort of searching for God has often been found to consist not so much in proactively doing things but in learning to be still, and in giving up the desire to control what and whom we are searching for. Advent is one of those times when it helps to practise waiting. We may think we know what we are waiting for, and we may be wrong.

Fainlight's poem starts with a very strict instruction to herself actually to stop searching. The assertion is that deliberate searching will result in a discovery which, whatever it is, will be 'wrong'. She is to 'sit/ Passive' – the pause over the line ending emphasizes the pause that the self must engage in. This, though the opposite of activity, is a struggle, the 'sternest trial of all'. Only emptiness of desire will attract what is the source of that desire – and by the end of this stanza, the 'other' who is sought is sensed as a 'wild, awkward child', stepping from the shadows because the stillness of the seeker finally makes that safe.

The second stanza focuses back on the superhuman internal struggle of the narrator to stay still and open, and allow this encounter to happen in a way that is not controlled by her own yearning. Passive and active images are juxtaposed in a way that conveys how powerful a paradoxical struggle is this emptiness. The narrator has to push 'against the grain' of her nature, which is actively to choose – so she has to push herself to refrain from pushing. The pain of this is captured well by the image of giving birth, a totally absorbing activity rightly described as 'labour', in which a woman is simultaneously required to wait an unconscionably long time for the desired outcome, and obliged to refrain from pushing at a crucial point when her entire body is straining to do so, in order for the baby to be safely delivered without tearing her.

The third stanza reverts to the image of the girl who, like a wild animal, will only approach if the seeker is utterly calm and still, even restraining her breathing – and who, one senses, could break away and vanish if there is any danger of being grabbed. The child has a puzzling stance; is the lifted arm a greeting or a defensive gesture to 'ward off attack'? The narrator is still speaking to herself sternly: 'I must hold myself back . . . I must even control . . .' But in the bracketed line it is as if a different tone of voice emerges – not severe but acknowledging more gently to herself how hard it is for her to know what she is seeing or what this encounter means.

In the final stanza there is a sense of unfolding recognition as the narrator finally hears a 'faint reedy voice'. The sense of struggle has dissolved, but the language here makes it hard for the reader to understand quite what or who is being precariously recognized. She recalls 'a language unspoken/ Since times before childhood' – what can this mean? Language is only developed within childhood, as a child grows out of infancy. Is this an image of an actual pre-birth connection (as with a twin who died in the womb or shortly after birth)? 'My forgotten sister' would suggest this interpretation. Or it might signify a part of herself that she has split off and denied. But there are echoes of God's knowledge of the self before birth (Psalm 139.13–16). This 'other' brings a message that she has had to wait 'so long to deliver' (presumably because the narrator, till now, has failed to wait or to listen). And to love her is to discover the self's 'own secret'.

What has been your most important experience of patient (or impatient) waiting?

7 December

————◆•◆•◆————

We grow accustomed to the Dark

We grow accustomed to the Dark –
When Light is put away –
As when the Neighbor holds the Lamp
To witness her Goodbye –

A Moment – We uncertain step
For newness of the night –
Then – fit our Vision to the Dark –
And meet the Road – erect –

And so of larger – Darknesses –
Those Evenings of the Brain –
When not a Moon disclose a sign –
Or Star – come out – within –

The Bravest – grope a little –
And sometimes hit a Tree
Directly in the Forehead –
But as they learn to see –

Either the Darkness alters –
Or something in the sight
Adjusts itself to Midnight –
And Life steps almost straight.

Emily Dickinson

An important dimension of Advent is that it moves through a time when the world is becoming increasingly dark. Days are shorter, night starts sooner, and the quality of the light is often dulled by poor weather. There is no avoiding having to live quite a large proportion of our waking life during hours of darkness, and for some people this is a physical reality that leads to gloom and even depression. Given our current usage of artificial light, perhaps the impact of December darkness is not as large for us as for earlier generations, but nevertheless it is still powerful. As we have observed in the collect for Advent Sunday (p. ix), Christian tradition has often emphasized a battle between the forces of light and darkness, with a very clear preference for the light. Yet engaging with the journey through the time of darkness may yield more than simply a sense of struggle against evil or threat of harm.

Emily Dickinson was a reclusive nineteenth-century poet with a distinctive voice. It is possible that one of the reasons for her introverted lifestyle may have been that she had a tendency to epilepsy. She also had prolonged treatment for her eyes, though it is not clear exactly what was wrong with them. Like Sylvia Plath she links her poetic vision to her physical sight. As in this poem, her work often references both the brain and ways of seeing, or not seeing. She has an extraordinary capacity to make remarks in her poetry that are apparently homely or conversational in tone, but which suddenly catapult the reader into an exploration of a reality that ranges from the unsettling to the frankly mystical. She does this here with the theme of darkness, which of course is a context in which we all, even when our vision is perfect, find that we have to deal with sightlessness and confusion.

The poem begins in a low-key way, referring to that common experience whereby we are particularly blinded by the dark when we have just been surrounded by light or gazing at a light source; however, the eyes adjust after a moment or two to reclaim their night vision. The poet speaks about that moment when a departing visitor turns away from the lamp that her neighbour has brought to the door to see her off, and she moves to find the way home. At a time when there was no electricity or domestic security lights on the doorstep, and minimum ambient light from gas-lit streetlamps in a semi-rural area, the darkness would have been palpable. It is, in a sense, an ordinary observation about a common experience, and yet there are hints of some other levels of meaning. This is what happens 'When Light is put away' – somehow this process feels larger than a simple flickering oil lamp. And the neighbour is described as holding the lamp 'To witness her Goodbye' – the choice of the word 'witness' feels formal and faintly religious.

However, the 'ordinary' tone continues, as the narrator describes the slight stumble that may well accompany that sudden sense of being seized by the 'newness of the night', the unreadiness of our sight to deal with the total lack of visual clues we momentarily experience. This stanza is still apparently describing this straightforward experience, although there is a growing sense that the act of fitting 'our Vision to the Dark' and meeting the road 'erect' may represent something deeper – about how we face the whole of our life – than simply retracing the path to our own house. Dickinson's characteristically odd use of capital letters and of dashes rather than usual punctuation tends to imply meanings that jolt strangely with surface reality.

Suddenly in the next verse we have stepped right into one of the potholes that the poet tends to produce; the effect is very like the stumble she has just been describing. 'And so of larger – Darknesses –/ Those Evenings of the Brain – '. Somehow an abyss of meaninglessness has opened up, in which outer and inner blindness (and terror) are experienced simultaneously, just with the use of ten common words. One way in which the poet achieves this is by referring quite casually to the comparison she is making, with the assumption that the reader knows very well what she is referring to. Whether or not it could be assumed that every reader is aware that we are always walking just on the verge of the abyss, they may grasp that now. The landscape of the night sky (so dominant where there is no light pollution) has become the map of the interior self. And neither moon nor stars are there to disclose anything of reality.

The narrator recognizes the fearfulness of this, and the courage required to face such darkness: 'The Bravest – grope a little'. Here we are once again back with the stumbling visitor who may even, in a slightly slapstick fashion, end up banging her head on the branch of a tree as she gets the path wrong. But at the same time we are in the company of contemplative saints across time who have embraced the way of 'unknowing', the *via negativa* or spiritual cloud of darkness that must be willingly entered in the search for God. At least, we may be. Dickinson doesn't afford us the luxury of being sure of any of her conceivably religious references.

Finally (and this is a surprisingly comforting ending for such a disconcerting poem), she allows the possibility either that the darkness accommodates us or that our own human vision adapts to embrace the dark. She offers us a last line which – apart from that painfully accurate word 'almost' – encourages us to believe that we can dare this.

Have you ever experienced the sense of being totally in the dark, either in your prayer life or in life decisions generally? Was it possible for you to risk keeping going in that darkness?

8 December

The Absence

It is this great absence
that is like a presence, that compels
me to address it without hope
of a reply. It is a room I enter

from which someone has just
gone, the vestibule for the arrival
of one who has not yet come.
I modernise the anachronism

of my language, but he is no more here
than before. Genes and molecules
have no more power to call
him up than the incense of the Hebrews

at their altars. My equations fail
as my words do. What resource have I
other than the emptiness without him of my whole
being, a vacuum he may not abhor?

R. S. Thomas

R. S. Thomas is a poet who, in the modern age, has perhaps done
more than anyone to explore both the lure and the intense difficulty
of prayer. Waiting on God, longing for a sense of God's presence,
keeping going when there seems to be hardly a sign of response,
are hallmarks of his work. While some of his poems do witness to
the occasional glorious baptism of grace – often at an unlooked-
for moment – many of them, like this one, speak powerfully of the

narrator's sense of God's absence, however earnestly sought. In this, he stands in the contemplative tradition of the *via negativa*, but with a helpful modern sensibility that this is not an esoteric path suitable for exceptional mystics only, but a well-trodden journey for so many Christians who find prayer just very tough going.

However, a sense of God's absence is a completely different thing from the sense that there is no God, and this vibrant emptiness is the subject of this poem. We start with stark paradoxes: the 'great absence' that is 'like a presence'; the something that 'compels' an address yet 'without hope/ of a reply'. An absence that can be thought of as having a size does imply its opposite. Someone who will not speak yet has somehow inspired prayer is definitely a reality, even if stubbornly silent or unresponsive. The introduction of 'hope', in a colloquial phrase that has theological resonances, makes us think of T. S. Eliot's meditation in 'East Coker' about waiting without hope. (This thought comes in a section that is all about going into the dark, 'Which shall be the darkness of God'.)

On the turn between the first and second stanzas, the poet tries a new image of the absence – the room that feels as if it has only at that moment been vacated (as it were, in the pause between our leaving one verse and entering the next). Then we are offered the corresponding image of the person who is awaited but has not yet arrived. The sense of 'just missing' someone is quickly married to the notion of expecting someone significant to turn up. The word 'vestibule' is very formal and a little archaic, implying an important visitor who is to be ushered into the presence chamber.

The poet deprecates his use of the 'anachronism' – but perhaps he is seeking to imply not just that his word was rather formal, but that the whole enterprise of waiting on God is a bit out of date, in modern understanding. He moves on to the contrasting idea that contemporary scientific ideas could be an additional resource for understanding God or finding ways to approach him. But he is obliged to admit that nothing he can bring to the exercise has any more power to compel God's response than the ancient methods involving incense and altars. Notice how the hopeless sentences wind around the line endings and the stanza breaks without a pause until this point.

'My equations fail/ as my words do.' It is here in the final stanza that the narrator's total failure is clearly announced. Nothing works; nothing compels God; words, equations, reasoning, all fail. There are no resources available to human beings that have the power to bring God down, make God hear our cry. The only resource is indeed the sheer human absence of resources: 'the emptiness without him of my whole/ being'. For the biblical witness is that God does hear the cry of those that have no power. The poem has counterposed the emptiness of the human heart with the 'great absence' that is God, so that they finally speak to each other.

The final line suggests that God not only hears but becomes truly present within the weak of the earth, choosing to empty himself in becoming incarnate as a human being. For the language, on the surface a wry reversal of the scientific principle that 'nature abhors a vacuum', also echoes the words of the famous carol, 'Lo, he abhors not the virgin's womb', and the Te Deum, 'thou didst not abhor the virgin's womb'. As ever with R. S. Thomas, it is only a question, not an assertion (but it is a passionate question that I think this time expects to be answered). But the one who prays is using the experience of Mary to demand a similar annunciation.

How much do you long to experience God's presence?

9 December

Dover Beach

The sea is calm to-night,
The tide is full, the moon lies fair
Upon the Straits; – on the French coast, the light
Gleams, and is gone; the cliffs of England stand,
Glimmering and vast, out in the tranquil bay.
Come to the window, sweet is the night air!
Only, from the long line of spray
Where the ebb meets the moon-blanch'd sand,
Listen! you hear the grating roar
Of pebbles, which the waves suck back, and fling,
At their return, up the high strand,
Begin, and cease, and then again begin,
With tremulous cadence slow, and bring
The eternal note of sadness in.

      Sophocles long ago
Heard it on the Aegaean, and it brought
Into his mind the turbid ebb and flow
Of human misery; we
Find also in the sound a thought,
Hearing it by this distant northern sea.

The sea of faith
Was once, too, at the full, and round earth's shore
Lay like the folds of a bright girdle furl'd;
But now I only hear
Its melancholy, long, withdrawing roar,
Retreating to the breath

Of the night-wind down the vast edges drear
And naked shingles of the world.

Ah, love, let us be true
To one another! for the world, which seems
To lie before us like a land of dreams,
So various, so beautiful, so new,
Hath really neither joy, nor love, nor light,
Nor certitude, nor peace, nor help for pain;
And we are here as on a darkling plain
Swept with confused alarms of struggle and flight,
Where ignorant armies clash by night.

Matthew Arnold

The period of Advent, which Elizabeth Jennings' poem (p. 5) describes as 'the season of right doubt', is an appropriate time to engage with the darkness and doubt that accompany the act of waiting. Matthew Arnold's poem is perhaps the most famous example of exploring loss of faith, which has been happening on a broad cultural scale (not just in the individual human heart) since the early nineteenth century. Phrases in this poem have been seized on as titles for books, or have inspired movements; the Sea of Faith Network is an interesting one, since it gathers people on the basis of having shaken off a literalistic belief in religious doctrines.

Some claim that Arnold drafted the poem on his honeymoon, in 1851. Given the poem's themes, this might seem an unusually gloomy mood to adopt on such an occasion, and it may be that this theory owes too much to the internal dramatic situation the poem implies. Arnold and his wife did honeymoon near Dover, and it could be imagined that the poem's monologue is conducted by a man to his new bride, gazing at the sea from the window of where they are staying. The poem was not published until 1867, some years after Charles Darwin's *On the Origin of Species* (1859), which had a huge impact on people's beliefs in the accuracy of the Bible's account of creation in Genesis (and it is worth noting that much of the coastline was being explored for fossils by amateur collectors). There had already been a major assault on people's unquestioning faith in the

Bible as a historical document, namely the investigation by German theologian David Strauss into the historical figure of Jesus (1835–36). This was translated by George Eliot (Marian Evans) in 1846 as *The Life of Jesus, Critically Examined*, and the shock waves of applying critical analysis to the figure of the Saviour had hit not just the churches but all of society. It may be hard for us to appreciate quite how painful and poignant an experience it must have been to wrestle with the challenge of the academy to what felt like the heart of faith.

But Arnold produced a remarkable poem which is perhaps the first 'free verse' work in the English language. It is not without structure, or indeed rhyme (though this is irregular), but it would have been received as remarkably experimental in its style at the time. This is partly why it seems to fit so well into a contemporary collection – it sounds modern. But the sentiments are profoundly Victorian, both in its aching sense of faith's departure, and in the Romantic notions that are the poem's only offering as a counterpoint for cultural despair.

The poem's form is that of a 'dramatic monologue' (the narrator is apparently speaking to another person, whose presence is assumed although they do not speak – so the reader is 'overhearing' one side of a conversation). The first stanza, describing a peaceful sea at full tide, with a full moon illuminating the iconic 'Glimmering and vast' white cliffs, paints an idyllic visual picture, like a holiday postcard scene. This is the untroubled scene that the bride is apparently called over to see. However, barely has the sweetness of the night air been praised when the worrying word 'Only' is introduced. The narrator now asks his bride to 'Listen!' The lovely seascape has an undertow of sounds that are not beautiful, and begin to have a menacing quality: 'the grating roar/ Of pebbles, which the waves suck back, and fling . .' Of course, the full tide is never a stationary thing. Whereas a seascape may look static and permanent from a distance, in reality there is an everchanging and restless interaction between the sea and the beach. This is something that can be heard, even if not detected by eye at a distance. Arnold makes full use of sibilant letters that echo the hiss and roar of the endlessly shifting pebbles: 'suck', 'strand', 'cease', 'cadence', 'sadness'.

The poem shifts from the seaward gaze of the lovers to thoughts of classical writers on distant Mediterranean shores. In a sense it is strange to shift centuries in this way, but Arnold was a classicist and it is not out of character for an overeducated young bridegroom, keen to improve his wife's understanding, to be comparing his own experience and poetic sensibility with that of one of Greece's greatest tragedians and explorers of the human psyche. It also has the effect of providing a context of centuries for the statement that is to come, since the poem starts to encompass the whole range of a Victorian's sense of the past, including our pre-Christian Western heritage.

The fourth stanza asserts the poignancy of a massive cultural loss of faith, and the images here are stunning. The second line carries on into the third in an unending way, reflecting the 'bright girdle' of faith like shining water encircling the earth – as it was perceived to do during the medieval period. 'Girdle' is a wonderful choice of word, suggesting both the flexible, extended beauty of the thing and the archaic quality of the costume it was part of. There is a correspondingly precise image of exposure when the garments of the faith are gone, leaving the 'naked shingles of the world'.

In the final stanza, the bridegroom turns to his love and asserts the sole capacity of Romantic love to conquer this loss – as much of popular culture has been doing ever since. It has to be said, however, that what the narrator goes on to list as the cruel disappointments of once-held certainties that are 'not really there' sound a great deal more convincing than the power of 'lurve'. The last few lines are almost Shakespearean in force, denying all reality to 'joy', 'love', 'light', 'certitude', 'peace', or even the minimal 'help for pain'. The poem abandons us simply with war, and war that is pointless, confused and self-destructive. No wonder it rings a bell with a contemporary age that has witnessed a century of world wars and repeated, sometimes random, acts of terror.

However, we may question how far we should simply identify the poet with the assertions of his narrator in this poem, especially as it is deliberately dramatic in construction. The young man could be seen as someone who rather luxuriates in Romantic extremes, whether it be the uplifting image of the poem's start or the bleak horror of its ending, on the 'darkling plain'. But it remains one of the most powerful expressions of the intensity of a loss of faith – as opposed to atheism or nihilism, which would suppose that the positive values listed were never anything but human wish-fulfilment.

From your own beliefs, what reply would you want to make to the last paragraph of the poem?

10 December

Church Going

Once I am sure there's nothing going on
I step inside, letting the door thud shut.
Another church: matting, seats, and stone,
And little books; sprawlings of flowers, cut
For Sunday, brownish now; some brass and stuff
Up at the holy end; the small neat organ;
And a tense, musty, unignorable silence,
Brewed God knows how long. Hatless, I take off
My cycle-clips in awkward reverence,

Move forward, run my hand around the font.
From where I stand, the roof looks almost new –
Cleaned, or restored? Someone would know: I don't.
Mounting the lectern, I peruse a few
Hectoring large-scale verses, and pronounce
'Here endeth' much more loudly than I'd meant.
The echoes snigger briefly. Back at the door
I sign the book, donate an Irish sixpence,
Reflect the place was not worth stopping for.

Yet stop I did: in fact I often do,
And always end much at a loss like this,
Wondering what to look for; wondering, too,
When churches fall completely out of use
What we shall turn them into, if we shall keep
A few cathedrals chronically on show,
Their parchment, plate and pyx in locked cases,

And let the rest rent-free to rain and sheep.
Shall we avoid them as unlucky places?

Or, after dark, will dubious women come
To make their children touch a particular stone;
Pick simples for a cancer; or on some
Advised night see walking a dead one?
Power of some sort or other will go on
In games, in riddles, seemingly at random;
But superstition, like belief, must die,
And what remains when disbelief has gone?
Grass, weedy pavement, brambles, buttress, sky,

A shape less recognisable each week,
A purpose more obscure. I wonder who
Will be the last, the very last, to see
This place for what it was; one of the crew
That tap and jot and know what rood-lofts were?
Some ruin-bibber, randy for antique,
Or Christmas-addict, counting on a whiff
Of gown-and-bands and organ-pipes and myrrh?
Or will he be my representative,

Bored, uninformed, knowing the ghostly silt
Dispersed, yet tending to this cross of ground
Through suburb scrub because it held unspilt
So long and equably what since is found
Only in separation – marriage, and birth,
And death, and thoughts of these – for which was built
This special shell? For, though I've no idea
What this accoutred frowsty barn is worth,
It pleases me to stand in silence here;

A serious house on serious earth it is,
In whose blent air all our compulsions meet,
Are recognised, and robed as destinies.
And that much never can be obsolete,
Since someone will forever be surprising

A hunger in himself to be more serious,
And gravitating with it to this ground,
Which, he once heard, was proper to grow wise in,
If only that so many dead lie round.

Philip Larkin

Larkin's twentieth-century poem provides an interesting contrast of tone with the preceding Victorian one. It is similarly exploring loss of faith, but its approach is undramatic and without the sense of pain and tragedy that we find in Arnold's poem. Instead of gloomy landscapes shot through with echoes of war, we are invited to consider the gradual decline in use of rural churches, as their shabby contemporary state seems to point to a future of actual ruins whose significance will bemuse people who stumble across them in centuries to come.

In spite of its theme, the poem has proved remarkably popular with churchgoers, and many have received it as a profoundly religious work in itself, much to Larkin's own annoyance. In an interview in 1964 he said, 'It is of course an entirely secular poem. I was a bit irritated by an American who insisted to me that it was a religious poem ... Of course the poem is about going to church, not religion – I tried to suggest this by the title – and the union of the important stages of human life – birth, marriage and death – that going to church represents; and my own feeling that when they are dispersed into the registry office and the crematorium chapel, life will become thinner in consequence' (in Philip Larkin, *The Complete Poems*, ed. Archie Burnett, Farrar, Straus and Giroux, 2012). The fact that we know about this discussion should not colour our reading of the poem too much. As D. H. Lawrence remarked (and Larkin himself mentions this quote): 'Never trust the artist. Trust the tale' (*Studies in Classical American Literature*, 1924, Chapter 1). A writer may not necessarily be the only or even the best critic of their own work, and may generate legitimate readings of which they are unaware.

It is a long, apparently conversational poem, in which nevertheless every word works hard. The narrator is someone who has made a habit of popping into little rural churches as he cycles round the countryside, and this particular church is depicted with excruciating accuracy, in all its banal ordinariness. 'Once I am sure there is nothing going on' – this casual introduction instantly cuts both ways. On the surface the caution of the polite visitor who is an outsider to any possible activities or services, it is also the observation that the state of the church generally is vacuous. The narrator seems clear-eyed about the depressing details: the 'little books', the 'sprawlings of flowers' that have died and not been removed, the unremarkable 'brass and stuff/ Up at the holy end'. Yet in spite of, or because of this, he responds to the 'tense, musty, unignorable silence,/ Brewed God knows how long'. Although he uses a mild colloquial blasphemy, God has been mentioned, and the silence itself (presumably the silence of centuries of faithful religious practice) has the power to prompt him to the rather comic 'awkward reverence' of removing his cycle-clips.

The second stanza watches him do what perhaps many who are the sole visitors to an empty church do: muse ignorantly about the architecture, try reading out from the lectern Bible, feel slightly accused by the unexpectedly loud echoes that 'snigger' as a result when the building is empty, leave a mean donation and 'reflect the place was not worth stopping for'. (The phrase 'worth stopping for' is famously the minimum recommendation in books about English churches. Churches with more architectural attractions might be 'worth a detour' or 'worth a journey'.)

But immediately in the third stanza the narrator turns and challenges himself: not that the church was worthy of a better grading, but that 'stop I did: in fact I often do'. It is his own continuing habit of visiting churches in an apparently desultory way that deserves investigation. He starts to fantasize where we are headed with church buildings. Taking for granted that they will eventually fall out of use, he imagines the most impressive being kept 'chronically on show' (hear the contempt for a tourism-only usage in that phrase, as in the alliteration applied to cathedral treasures of 'parchment, plate and pyx'). The others he sees being let 'rent-free to rain and sheep'. He begins a thought, continued in the next verse, that a superstitious usage of the buildings will arise: fearful avoidance; particular stones being thought of as 'lucky'; graveyards as places to pick herbal remedies, or spot ghosts on particular nights. Then he sees even the power of superstition disappearing: 'what remains when disbelief has gone?/ Grass, weedy pavement, brambles, buttress, sky.' The last line has a bleak power; it is true that the monuments of much older religions in our landscape have gone this way, and left no sure access to the meanings they originally held.

Then the narrator asks who will be the very last visitor to the church who actually knows something of what its original purpose was. The language used here is very dismissive. He speaks of the 'crew/ That tap and jot and know what rood-lofts were', the 'ruin-bibber', the 'Christmas-addict' – note that he mentions only those whose interest is history or antique practices, not actual worshippers. He contrasts these parasitic, addictive collector types with the imagined future person like himself who, while alienated and uninformed, finds that it pleases him 'to stand in silence here', because this rather terrible old barn was created to contain and dignify important human milestones like birth, marriage and death.

Although the whole poem, in the separate words of its title and throughout its length, assumes that the 'church' is 'going', the final stanza comes down with a surprisingly beautiful assertion of the importance of what these buildings hold and represent. In spite of Larkin's own view of the poem, it is hard not to hear this verse as some sort of statement of serious trust in something that could only have been created by religious practice, which recognizes our human needs and robes them 'as destinies'. Or, if not a statement as such, it is something that puzzles the narrator and gives him serious pause. And I defy anyone to reach the last line without coming close to tears.

Do you think this is a religious poem, or not? What is it that draws you to the Church? And what tends to disappoint you there?

11 December

———•◦•———

Ozymandias

I met a traveller from an antique land
Who said: Two vast and trunkless legs of stone
Stand in the desert . . . Near them, on the sand,
Half sunk, a shattered visage lies, whose frown,
And wrinkled lip, and sneer of cold command,
Tell that its sculptor well those passions read
Which yet survive, stamped on these lifeless things,
The hand that mocked them, and the heart that fed:
And on the pedestal these words appear:
'My name is Ozymandias, king of kings:
Look on my works, ye Mighty, and despair!'
Nothing beside remains. Round the decay
Of that colossal wreck, boundless and bare
The lone and level sands stretch far away.

P. B. Shelley

This famous sonnet by another avowed unbeliever provides an interesting comparison with the previous poem by Philip Larkin, as it also deals with the impact of the passage of time on the meanings carried by human constructions. This poem depicts an existing ruin, and invites the reader to look back in time to the intentions of the sculptor and the person who commissioned it – and then to perceive the ironic contrast between the arrogant pretensions of the ancient king and the present-day state of his ruined likeness. Originally written in 1818 as a passionate critique of monarchy, it contains some interesting biblical resonances and is fruitful to study in

Advent as we reflect on the nature of the kingship of Christ, compared with human tyrannies.

Shelley was born and raised as an aristocrat, but developed radical views at an early age. He was seriously bullied at Eton and was expelled from Oxford for publishing atheist views. In his own generation he was dismissed as a dangerous radical (the fallout from the French Revolution caused shock waves in the English aristocracy), but he became a hero for several generations of Romantic and radical poets. 'Ozymandias' was written in competition with his friend Horace Smith, who published a poem on a similar theme only a month after Shelley. It seems to be based on his knowledge of the historical writings of Diodorus Siculus about Ramesses II of Egypt (whose name was transliterated in Greek to Ozymandias). At the same time there was excitement in Europe about a recently discovered statue of that pharaoh, which was eventually acquired by the British Museum, after Napoleon had attempted, but failed, to secure it. So, although Shelley cannot have seen the statue when he wrote the poem (and the opening lines bear witness to this), he would have heard about it in a context where kings and emperors were fascinated by such icons of kingly power.

The poem is formally a sonnet, but it has a very unusual pattern of rhymes that interweave, so that the impression is more conversational than such a carefully constructed form might suggest. It is written as a traveller's tale, and a good deal of it seems to be simply describing what was seen, without comment. There is no heavy-handed pointing of the moral, and yet its power of critique is immense.

The picture is painted slowly for the reader's imagination. First we are introduced to the 'vast and trunkless legs of stone'. The colossal impact of what we might be asked to see is immediately undercut by the absurdity of the thought of legs that have no body to support. The 'sand' on which the face of the statue is found is the only indication at this stage of the desert where it was seen. Significantly, the 'visage' is already 'shattered' and lies 'Half sunk'. So the first information we are given about this statue is that it is broken. But it is also implied that it shows someone who used to hold authority, of a cruel and arrogant kind. The details of the statue's 'wrinkled lip, and sneer of cold command' suggest that it is easy to examine these features close up, in their detached and humiliated position on the ground.

The narrator then offers the only explicit comment of interpretation in the poem: the judgement that the sculptor has conveyed accurately the passions of the king who commissioned this work, since the broken stones, 'these lifeless things', still have the power to communicate 'command'. But we are reminded that the king now is truly a lifeless thing with less power than the stones that were shaped to represent him. 'The hand that mocked them' refers to the sculptor's skill in representing the subject's passions, since 'mock' could mean to create an imitation (as in mock-up). It also carries the double meaning of 'ridicule' – even the sculptor who worked to order could by his accuracy reflect the absurdities of tyranny. 'The heart that fed' refers to the king's arrogant heart that fuelled his dreams of omnipotence.

As we enter the sestet – the last six lines of the sonnet traditionally offer a 'turn' in the meaning, which interprets what has been set out in the first eight lines – the narrator returns to his description. First there is the boasting inscription, announcing the king's name and legacy, with accompanying threat to his enemies. Then there is the simple assertion that 'Nothing beside remains'. Finally, the desert mentioned at the start of the poem is described properly, so that our inward eye is taken outward from focusing on the ruin of the statue to the endless and empty sands that are its context now. There are no works; there is no legacy; nobody knows or cares about the so-called 'king of kings' with the fancy five-syllabled name; he has no power to make anyone despair. The empty arrogance of monarchs is laid bare, as well as the stupidity of contemporary tyrants who seek to bolster their own status by acquiring antique statues that embody it.

One of the reasons why the image explored in this poem has such power is the biblical echoes around it. The book of Daniel, an apocalyptic work that is traditionally read in the weeks before Christmas, tells first of a dream about a mighty image and then of an actual statue of gold that everyone is required to bow down to and worship, on pain of death. Nebuchadnezzar's dream, which Daniel interprets, shows a statue of mixed materials (including the famous feet of clay) which will be utterly destroyed by a stone 'cut from a mountain by no human hand' (Daniel 2.45). Then Nebuchadnezzar sets up a golden image, but Daniel and his friends openly defy the law and refuse to worship it. The three friends are thrown into 'the burning fiery furnace' (Daniel 3.21) but are kept safe by God and delivered from death. In the biblical context the story is a witness against the worship of idols; but it is clear that this usually means refusing to accept the power of earthly kings.

After the time of Christ, many decades passed before he was depicted in art at all, whether as a shepherd, a suffering saviour, a holy infant or a reigning monarch. One of the earliest images that pointed to his identity was that of the king-defying 'three holy children' in the fiery furnace, who are accompanied by a fourth presence which seems to be divine (Daniel 3.25), and which early Christians identified as Christ himself. A strong tradition about reflecting on 'Christ the King' as we approach the story of his birth is to try and grasp how utterly different is the kingship of the true 'king of kings' from the temporarily powerful monarchs or other world leaders who effectively but illegitimately claim this title. Shelley may not have been a Christian believer, but Christian faith demands a similarly radical critique of tyranny.

How far does your understanding of Christ's kingship influence how you yourself exercise power, or stand up to abuses of power?

12 December

The Second Coming

Turning and turning in the widening gyre
The falcon cannot hear the falconer;
Things fall apart; the centre cannot hold;
Mere anarchy is loosed upon the world,
The blood-dimmed tide is loosed, and everywhere
The ceremony of innocence is drowned;
The best lack all conviction, while the worst
Are full of passionate intensity.

Surely some revelation is at hand;
Surely the Second Coming is at hand.
The Second Coming! Hardly are those words out
When a vast image out of *Spiritus Mundi*
Troubles my sight: somewhere in sands of the desert
A shape with lion body and the head of a man,
A gaze blank and pitiless as the sun,
Is moving its slow thighs, while all about it
Reel shadows of the indignant desert birds.
The darkness drops again; but now I know
That twenty centuries of stony sleep
Were vexed to nightmare by a rocking cradle,
And what rough beast, its hour come round at last,
Slouches towards Bethlehem to be born?

W. B. Yeats

Deeply embedded in the mood of Advent is meditation not solely
on the coming of the Christchild, either centuries ago or coming

to human hearts today, but on the promised/threatened 'second coming', the end time, the apocalypse, the time of final judgement. For some Christians in our own generation, this expectation is paramount in their spirituality, and a literal 'rapture' of the saints is daily anticipated (there are websites set up to estimate the prevalence of signs of the coming rapture). The huge popularity of the 'Left Behind' series of novels, which envisages just such an event, witnesses to genuine conviction that it will happen, and happen soon; arguably some US policies in recent decades have been influenced by this belief. For many other Christians, this seems like nonsense with no more plausibility than alleged Mayan predictions that the world was due to end on 21 December 2012. But there is a strong tradition of the 'end-time' woven into the Gospels as well as the Hebrew Scriptures and it seems that early Christians believed that they were the last generation alive before Christ's return.

What does it mean to inhabit this expectation and this apocalyptic imagery in our contemporary world, and allow real force to the sense that we and the whole of creation will stand before the throne of judgement? Yeats wrote his poem 'The Second Coming' in 1919, just in the aftermath of the First World War. The world had just experienced the nearest imaginable thing to a global apocalypse, with millions upon millions dead or displaced, followed by a horrendous flu epidemic that was claiming the lives of many more young people. Half a generation had indeed been wiped out; whole cultures lay devastated and their surviving citizens stunned and scarred. The Russian Revolution had erupted, and in Yeats' Ireland the Easter Rising and massacre had happened, with unknowable consequences. If any combination of occurrences in world history could be taken as an unmistakable sign of the end of all things, this was it.

Yeats starts with a series of his own images of the falling apart of all meaning: the falcon (a bird of prey) rising on an ever-widening spiral, away from the sound and controlling arm of the falconer (a medieval image of stability that is now beyond recall); the collapse of the 'centre' of the traditional universe; the loosing on the world not of disciplined armies but of 'mere anarchy'; a tide of blood that drowns everything, especially innocence, and any communal celebrations that used to have an innocent feel. All activities are tainted with blood (there are echoes of the bloody seas of the book of Revelation, 8.8). In public life, political parties and politicians who might normally command respect 'lack all conviction' (does this mean that they are unconvincing or that they have no real principles?). And then there are the others – the totally convinced and very influential movements that harness a 'passionate intensity', but to fanatical and violent ends.

The second part of the poem introduces, in an almost breathless series of exclamations, the thought that the Second Coming, whatever that means, must be at hand. But this idea gives rise to an image that is troubling, and menacing. It is not an image of clarity or judgement (however severe), but is partially bestial, and with no clearer meaning than the lost falcon, or the anarchic tide of blood. I wonder if there are some echoes of and contrasts with Shelley's poem here, as Yeats depicts a desert scene where an ancient and apparently static presence (the sphinx, with the lion's body and the human head) ceases to be an irrelevant antiquity and comes gradually but terrifyingly to life. The human part of the creature, its face, is 'blank and pitiless as the sun'; the animal part moves 'its slow thighs' in the manner of a lion quietly beginning the hunt. And the vigilant 'desert birds' notice the beginning of an attack, however noiselessly the creature stalks.

Whatever the ending means, it is a vision of an ancient godlike creature, captured in stone and presiding over the desert for 2,000 years, turning into an image of the Second Coming as the arrival of a 'rough beast', not a child in the manger and not a Christ in glory. Where does this concept spring from? There are biblical prophecies that depict God as a ferocious lion (Amos 3.8), even one who rends and tears his people before he heals them (Hosea 5.14). There are other prophecies (Revelation 13.1–4) where the image of the 'beast' is most certainly not an image of God but of his adversary. The last line of the poem chillingly asks a question that makes the reader reflect on what it means to look towards Bethlehem; what kind of God is really coming?

Is the expectation of a second coming a significant part of your faith? If so, how does it affect your decisions and political beliefs now?

13 December

The Tyger

Tyger Tyger, burning bright,
In the forests of the night;
What immortal hand or eye,
Could frame thy fearful symmetry?

In what distant deeps or skies,
Burnt the fire of thine eyes?
On what wings dare he aspire?
What the hand, dare sieze the fire?

And what shoulder, & what art,
Could twist the sinews of thy heart?
And when thy heart began to beat,
What dread hand? & what dread feet?

What the hammer? what the chain,
In what furnace was thy brain?
What the anvil? what dread grasp,
Dare its deadly terrors clasp?

When the stars threw down their spears
And water'd heaven with their tears:
Did he smile his work to see?
Did he who made the Lamb make thee?

Tyger Tyger burning bright,
In the forests of the night:
What immortal hand or eye,
Dare frame thy fearful symmetry?

William Blake

The preceding poem by Yeats ends with the vision of a menacing 'rough beast' whose time has come to be born into the world. It could hardly fail to owe something to the creature in Blake's poem 'The Tyger', which has been perhaps the most anthologized and analysed poem in the English language.

'The Tyger' (tradition retains the archaic spelling, perhaps to signal that this is about rather more than a large feline predator) was published in 1794 as part of *Songs of Experience*. This balanced Blake's earlier sequence *Songs of Innocence*, a blend that he described on the title page as 'Shewing the two Contrary States of the Human Soul'. The poem directly corresponds to his earlier poem 'The Lamb', which gives additional weight to the question at the end of the fifth stanza, 'Did he who made the Lamb make thee?' While arguments continue to rage as to what the poem is all about, this question inevitably focuses on the nature of God as creator. Both poems have been set to music by the modern composer John Tavener: 'The Lamb' is a beautiful carol often heard at seasonal concerts and services; however, I do not think his setting of 'The Tyger' is likely to be heard in churches during the approach to Christmas. And yet its apocalyptic tone and insistent questions about theodicy (why does evil exist if there is a God of love?) are in my view appropriate to Advent reflection in the 'season of right doubt'. When will we as Christians engage with what is fearful in creation or in the divine if not during this annual descent into the dark?

The poem begins with repetition, like a children's nursery rhyme, and it continues with an utterly regular rhythm and simple strong rhyme scheme that makes it easy to learn. Indeed, in the past children were often given it to learn by heart, though the subject matter, when spelled out, is deeply troubling to adults. The rhythm, which stresses line endings and often the mid-line as well, functions like a drumbeat on the mind, reflecting the sinister heartbeat ('when thy heart began to beat') of a creature that – like Frankenstein's monster – someone has chosen to create and let loose upon the world. The poem gets unforgettably into the reader's brain, and not in a good way.

The setting for the poem is 'the forests of the night'. Putting it this way makes the 'night' primary and the 'forests' metaphorical: we are in the kingdom of darkness, not in a realistic forest at night time. The Tyger is 'burning bright'. This is a reference to the orange stripes of a tiger's fur, or perhaps to its searing yellow eyes, but it also suggests a force and presence – possibly demonic (like Lucifer the light-bringer and fallen angel). Immediately the question is asked about the creator of such a beast. 'Symmetry', which crucially underlies the sense of beauty in nature, is here applied to the terror of those symmetrical stripes. 'Frame' might mean fashioning or creating the beast, but it might also suggest containment (or its impossibility).

By the beginning of the next verse it seems clear that we are in the territory of the book of Job, which Blake frequently quarried for inspiration in both his poetry and his illustrations. Job, whom God allows to be tested almost to destruction by adversity, comes to a point where he challenges God's ordering of the world for allowing such evil, with a daring and an anger rarely seen in religious texts. God's 'answer' to Job in the book is to point to the realm of the created world, including those monstrous creatures who are created by God but whose ways are beyond the understanding of human beings. But the last line of this verse, 'What the hand, dare sieze the fire?' seems also to remind us of the classical myth of Prometheus, who stole the secret of fire from the gods to give human beings warmth, and was eternally punished for his feat. To the Romantic movement he became the icon of the one who dares everything for the sake of creativity.

Blake's cosmology included viewing God the Creator as like a master craftsman or blacksmith. This idea is powerfully present in the next two stanzas, which transform the action of seizing fire into the image of the smith's furnace, the dangerous place where powerful hands and shoulders wield the tools that can shape, twist, hammer and forge molten metal into new shapes that may be deadly. The poem draws attention to the intense physicality of the Tyger: eyes, sinews, heart, brain. But this is mixed with reference to the body of the creator who is forging these: 'What the hand', 'what shoulder', 'What dread hand? and what dread feet?', 'what dread grasp'. We notice that the qualities of the Tyger are also attributed to the one who makes the beast – the word 'dread' now belongs to the creator and not just his creation.

In the fifth verse we have the reversals of the traditional creation myths. In Job, the act of creation is accompanied by a shout of praise: 'the morning stars sang together, and all the sons of God shouted for joy' (Job 38.7); but here they weep and throw down their spears. In Genesis, when each part of creation is complete, it is said that 'God saw that it was good' (Genesis 1). Can the same be said for the creation of a thing like the Tyger? 'Did he smile his work to see?' is a truly chilling question, suggesting perhaps even a sadistic satisfaction in the creation of a stunningly beautiful killing machine, compared to a harmless and innocent creature like a lamb. Finally the first verse is repeated, with the single change of word: 'Could' becomes 'Dare'. What kind of God is the God of all creation? What risks is he prepared to take?

How do you reconcile a loving God with the more terrible aspects of creation?

14 December

————•◦•————

Darkness
after Rilke

Darkness,
your grand circle engulfs
all the small bright circles
of the world. None
can withstand you:
meteors trailing their lights
through space, this slim
candle on a shelf.
All selves
belong to you, began
in you. You place
a hand on my shoulder, shift
hand to wrist, feel my pulse.
Your gentleness moves
me to belief: in
darkness.

Alan Payne

Advent begins with a prayer for grace to 'cast away the works of darkness' (p. ix), and it is normal in Christian liturgy to use darkness as a metaphor for evil or as a cloak for the actions of those who are plotting evil. However, there is another strand of tradition that is comfortable with the image of darkness, viewing it as a place where God may be sought and found. On this day in December, very close to the darkest time of the year in the northern hemisphere, the Church celebrates the sixteenth-century Spanish mystic St John of the Cross, whose most famous love poem to God is entitled 'La noche oscura' ('The Dark Night').

Alan Payne's poem 'Darkness' takes its inspiration from a more modern poet, who works with the image of the dark as the source of all life and creativity. It was written after a discussion in a poetry group of a whole range of English versions of Rilke's brief poem 'Du Dunkelheit'. The sheer volume of attempted translations witnesses to the lure and popularity of this poem; but it is hard to translate from the German, partly because inevitably the wordplay gets lost in the transfer to English, but also because it is quite obscure exactly what Rilke understands the darkness to be. Rilke was raised as a Catholic (and was no doubt aware of the contemplative traditions that celebrated darkness), but he explicitly rejected his faith, even refusing to see a priest on his deathbed. At the same time he was influenced by the psychoanalytic concepts of Jung and Freud that were beginning to gain currency when he was writing. He once wrote to a younger poet in terms that suggest that for him darkness was the source of his own poetic creativity, a force with which he totally identified, and to which he had to surrender in order to access his poetic inspiration.

What Payne has written is not a direct translation of 'Du Dunkelheit': some images in the German poem are omitted, and some new ones introduced, and the shape of the poem is different. But Payne is clear that this new poem is 'after Rilke', seeking to capture important elements of the spirit of Rilke's poem.

It begins with a direct address to 'Darkness', whose name inhabits the whole first line; and indeed the poem ends with the same word, completing a circle which reflects the larger and smaller circles mentioned in the poem. 'Grand circle' has a large, all-encompassing ring to it, also suggesting the warmth and excitement of the grand circle in a theatre. Theatres, of course, work by harnessing the power of darkness within the auditorium. The 'small bright circles' held within the larger circle could be theatre lights, capable of dimming or brightening, that contribute to the coherent performance of the whole. But since these are 'of the world', the panorama shifts to a more cosmic plane, and the reader is suddenly aware that what we think of as the realm of light may shrink to just tiny circles of light within an unimaginably vast universe of blackness.

The mention of meteors trailing faint tails of light makes this plain. Moving from meteor to candle ought in principle to have an effect of huge contrast, but I think it is the opposite. The juxtaposition with the 'slim/ candle' (a wonderfully precise adjective to call forth the visual image) actually makes the meteor seem comparably tiny, in the depths of space. Darkness has all power: 'None/ can withstand you'.

At the mid-point of the poem there is a kind of turn, with the assertion that forms the core of this text: 'All selves/ belong to you, began/ in you.' The partnership of the two words starting with 'be' emphasizes the role of darkness as the alpha and omega of existence, consciousness and selfhood – not just for humanity but for all creatures. Then there is a highly intimate image of touch (appropriate for darkness, in which by definition the visual sense has no clues to offer). Darkness, directly addressed as 'you', is imagined as a person (a lover or friend? a parent? a doctor?) whose hand is felt on shoulder, wrist and pulse – noticing and affirming the evidence of life, but perhaps also quite seductive. This image has resonances of St John of the Cross, and the night 'that joined the lover to the beloved' ('La noche oscura', verse 5). There may also be echoes of Psalm 139.4: 'Thou dost beset me behind and before, and layest thy hand upon me.'

The end of the poem is a statement of faith: faith in darkness itself. Interestingly, Rilke's darkness is perhaps less clearly human than Payne's; it is more of a 'force', lacking the human touch that we find here. The word 'gentleness' confirms the sense of warmth and security introduced right at the beginning; this is darkness one can trust, and safely surrender oneself to.

Are you comfortable with the idea of God as one who can be found in darkness, as well as in the light?

15 December

Blackbird in Fulham

A John the Baptist bird which comes before
The light, chooses an aerial
Toothed like a garden rake, puts a prong at each shoulder,
Opens its beak and becomes a thurifer
Blessing dark above dank holes between the houses,
Sleek patios or rag-and-weed-choked messes.

Too aboriginal to notice these,
Its concentration is on resonance
Which excavates in sleepers memories
Long overgrown or expensively paved-over,
Of innocence unmawkish, love robust.
Its sole belief, that light will come at last.

The point is proved and, casual, it flies elsewhere
To sing more distantly, as though its tune
Is left behind imprinted on the air,
Still legible, though this the second carbon.
And puzzled wakers lie and listen hard
To something moving in their minds' backyard.

P. J. Kavanagh

In this poem we return to the traditional notion that it is light that is the place of life, energy and hope. As in the poem by Sylvia Plath (p. 16), the catalyst for illumination is a bird – this time the blackbird, which is always the first voice in the dawn chorus. The bird's activity, so acutely observed here, is most noticeable in early spring rather than in December, but this poem is often chosen as an Advent meditation because of the comparison made between the blackbird and John the Baptist – both are heralds of the light.

It is a 'John the Baptist bird' because of the Church's celebration of John especially during Advent as the forerunner of the Christ. In the Gospels, much is made of the significance of John, and many stories show him pointing to the coming of the Messiah, and recognizing Jesus as being that person. Most important here is the prologue of John's Gospel, which speaks of Jesus as the light of the world, and John, 'a man sent from God' as his witness (John 1.6–8). John is a strange and insistent figure in the Gospels, whose teaching and baptizing stir people to repent their sins and make changes in their life (Luke 3.1–14).

The poem attributes precise intention to the blackbird – intention related to its effect on the human beings who hear it. Of course, in reality the bird is establishing its territory against other blackbirds, and seems to get going while it is still dark in order to create a powerful 'sound presence' even before it is visible. But here, the bird is seen; it 'chooses an aerial', positioning itself with care between the teeth. Blackbirds do seem to like to occupy the highest point of a building or tree, and this twig-like arrangement makes a good vantage point. Even in the half light, the silhouette of the bird and the aerial can be observed. It 'puts a prong at each shoulder' (that is where the prongs end up because of where it perches, but the words suggest that the bird, consciously about to perform, arranges the matter itself).

Then it 'Opens its beak and becomes a thurifer', as if these movements and singing are part of deliberate liturgy of praise or invocation. A thurifer is the person who handles the incense-burner in Catholic high mass liturgies, with which Kavanagh would have been familiar. It is a skilled role, and involves swinging the thurible, a metal container holding hot coals and incense, on its chain constantly, so that the fire is maintained and the incense keeps smoking its fragrance reliably to accompany the progress of the service. At key moments the smoke of the incense is directed variously towards the altar, the priest or the congregation as a gesture of blessing. It is as if the song of the blackbird does something similar to the patches of ground beneath him, encompassing all sorts of locations, whether impressive 'Sleek patios' or messy gardens and 'dank holes between the houses'. This is a brilliant image of the blackbird's song, not only because of the associations of ritual blessing, but because the song does seem to keep going continuously without a break, like the action of the incense-bearer.

So within the first few lines the poem has already placed us both in the specific location of a variety of back gardens in Fulham just before dawn, and, it is implied, in the realm of human lives, whether chaotic or ordered, poverty-stricken or wealthy, which are all equally offered an unasked-for blessing from above, announcing the hope of light. After the pause of a line break, the narrator momentarily pulls back from this highly conscious role attributed to the blackbird, and acknowledges that it is 'too aboriginal' to take note of garden design, being focused on the production of its own resonant sound. But then the image of the differently maintained gardens is worked again for its capacity to image the human heart and mind. The song 'excavates' the memories of the people sleeping beneath it, 'Long overgrown or expensively paved-over'. The suggestion is that some memories of great significance may get overlaid and buried either through neglect or through the veneer of success and riches. These are the direct childhood memories of 'innocence unmawkish, love robust' – unlike, it is implied, the nostalgia of adulthood and its unstable loves.

We return to the blackbird, and its intense conviction that 'light will come at last'. The half-rhyme of 'last' with 'robust', with their strong endings, suggests that the blackbird holds its beliefs a lot more simply and single-mindedly than we do. Immediately 'The point is proved' (in fact light is dawning, just as the bird's song has seemed to promise). The narrator then depicts the bird flying to another vantage point, where it can still be heard pouring out its endless song, but more distantly. The image is of the song being 'imprinted on the air' in the place where the poem is set, still reverberating although the bird has flown further away so the actual sound is fainter. This effect is described here as the 'second carbon' – an image that will be familiar only to those who remember old-fashioned typewriters. When all office letters were typed mechanically, the only way to create file copies was to insert a thin sheet of paper beneath the top sheet, with a carbon paper between them. This was clean on one side and inked on the other, and as you typed it created a fainter copy on the sheet beneath. You could just about do two copies using two carbons, but the copy created by the 'second carbon' was very fuzzy and faint. This is the image of the 'Still legible' but much fainter song described in the poem.

The last two lines finally mention the human beings whose sleepy, almost awake presence has been implied throughout. It is only when the blessing of the 'full power' song has been received, and is now receding and difficult to 'read', that they begin to attend properly to what is going on, and what the birdsong has stirred or excavated in their memories. In a brilliant final use of the 'garden' image, the poet suggests the emergence of something (perhaps a kind of hope?) 'moving in their minds' backyard'. This sense, not overstated but beautifully implied, speaks of a kind of Advent readiness to receive the blessing and mystery that may be drawing near. For, as the responses that are repeated at morning prayer during Advent proclaim: 'Now is the time to awake out of sleep' (echoing Romans 13.11).

In what state is the 'backyard' of your mind and heart? ('Long overgrown or expensively paved-over'?) What needs to happen before the song of blessing can be fully received by you?

16 December

The Bat

I was reading about rationalism,
the kind of thing we do up north
in early winter, where the sun
leaves work for the day at 4:15.

Maybe the world *is* intelligible
to the rational mind;
and maybe we light the lamps at dusk
for nothing. . . .

Then I heard wings overhead.

The cats and I chased the bat
in circles – living room, kitchen,
pantry, kitchen, living room. . . .
At every turn it evaded us

like the identity of the third person
in the Trinity: the one
who spoke through the prophets,
the one who astounded Mary
by suddenly coming near.

Jane Kenyon

Jane Kenyon was a New England poet who wrote spare, allusive
poems that combine acute observations of rural life with religious
references that are often surprising and are tantalizingly momen-
tary. The reader usually has plenty of work to do to grasp exactly
what the insight might mean. This text opens a sequence of poems

in this book that in one way or another focus on the extraordinary event that ushers in the Incarnation – the annunciation, or visit by the angel to Mary, to invite her cooperation with heaven. As Advent progresses it is traditional to celebrate the role played by Mary in the drama of salvation, and to reflect on how we too may be approached by the divine in the midst of ordinary life.

The poem opens in a conversational way, introducing the subject of the narrator's reading matter, 'rationalism'. Apparently random and a matter of happenstance, of course the theme provides the contrast with the later musings about matters on which rationalism is necessarily silent. The narrator seems to feel that her reading tastes will be heard as pretentious, and so deflates this impression in a semi-ironic way (which nevertheless implies, as it would do in a British context, that northerners are not the uneducated plebs that they are sometimes taken for). It is 'the kind of thing we do up north/ in early winter'. So the poet, in a very few words, has located the speaker and identified her defensive pride in her identity. The reference to the sun who 'leaves work for the day at 4:15' is precise about the depths of winter as the solstice approaches, and also perhaps suggests a stereotype that northerners clock off work early in similar fashion.

The next stanza sees the narrator musing on the principles she is reading about, willing to concede that they may be an adequate description of the world we live in – though it is not very plausible that lighting the lamps at dusk is 'for nothing', in a rural context where the ambient darkness is profound. Perhaps the reference is to needless fears prompted by being in the dark; if there is nothing there beyond the rational, there is nothing to be afraid of or surprised by.

Then there is a single line, which is the centre and crux of the poem: 'Then I heard wings overhead.' We have been primed to expect something that contradicts rational understanding. But it is quickly made clear that this isn't an angel, but a bat that has somehow got into the house (perhaps it has awoken from hibernation and is confused). The recognition is not spelt out; we move straight to a comic description of a mad bat-chase through the rooms of the house, listed in a circular manner as the spooked narrator and her frenzied cats make futile efforts to match the speed of the bat as it quickly flutters, never still and not quite visible, back and forth through the accommodations. 'At every turn it evaded us', as the creature would.

But then, on the turn of the line break and the move to the next stanza, the poem lurches into quite different territory, and one much greater than an angel enters the poem. The simile produced is startling but, given the distinctive flying behaviour of bats, oddly appropriate: 'like the identity of the third person/ in the Trinity'. This person is not named, but it is the Holy Spirit (or in traditional language, perhaps particularly relevant to this experience, 'Holy Ghost'). The enigmatic Spirit, doctrinally the other party, with Mary, in the conception of Jesus, has often been associated with a dove (for example, Luke 3.22), and some cultures have seen other birds as the Spirit's emblem (such as the wild goose in the western isles of Scotland). But the comparison with a bat is arresting and quite unusual – perhaps unique.

Making the reference in formal theological language has the effect of referring back to the narrator's interestingly intellectual reading matter. It's clear that we have moved into a different discipline and universe of discourse, but there is a way of talking about this experience in academic terms. Next we are pointed specifically to the major confessional statement of the Church, the Nicene Creed, where it is asserted that the Holy Spirit has spoken 'through the prophets'. And finally, and here the poem ends, we are left with the personal impact of the Holy Spirit on Mary: 'the one who astounded Mary/ by suddenly coming near'. All the panic and surprise of the contemporary bat-chase described earlier is packed into that well-chosen word 'astounded'.

So the rather intellectual narrator is shown moving through academic definition, and formal credal statement, to a visceral reaction to a visitation from God, who may, like a bewildering bat, 'suddenly come near'.

What is your own experience of the action of the Holy Spirit?

17 December

Annunciation

When first he painted the Virgin the friar filled
the space around her with angels' wings,
scalloped and plated, with skies of gold,

heavy with matter. He thought that he knew
that heaven was everywhere. He grew
older, wiser and found that he drew

more homely rooms with pots and beds,
but lavished his art on soft furnishings
and the turn of the waiting angel's wings

(still gorgeous with colour and precious dust).
Much later, he sensed that his God had withdrawn,
was spacious. On smaller frescoes he painted less,

let wall be wall, but drew in each lawn
the finer detail of sorrel and weeds.
Still later, he found his devotion drawn

to nothing – shadows hinted at hidden rooms,
at improbable arches, while the angel's news
shattered the Virgin, who became a view

as open as virtue, her collapsing planes
easy and vacant as the evening breeze
that had brought a plain angel to his grateful knees.

Gwyneth Lewis

This poem depends on renaissance images of the moment of the annunciation. Although it does not name him, the poem charts the way that the Dominican friar Fra Angelico (1400–55) depicted this theme over his lifetime, on frescoes and altarpieces. Through examining the changing practice of this remarkable painter, Gwyneth Lewis asks the reader to enter into different levels of encounter with the subject. Interestingly, she observes that it is a process of becoming more spare, more ordinary, more austere, as the friar seeks to get to grips with the mystery of Incarnation. Lewis has written the poem as part of a sequence of six that are, as she puts it, 'on Nothing'.

The poem is a series of seven three-line stanzas, which move smoothly on over the line breaks and the gaps between verses, as if the maturing devotion of Fra Angelico is a seamless process. There are frequent end-rhymes that echo one another, but these are not regular, so a low-key conversational tone is maintained.

The first verse describes the very lush, complex paintings first produced by the young friar, with lavish use of gold leaf on the angels' wings and sky. Notice the emphasis given to the effect of the sheer weight of glowing paintwork: it is 'heavy with matter' – the phrase is given a weighty place at the start of the second verse. The interpretation offered already includes its own sense of uncertainty: 'He thought that he knew/ that heaven was everywhere.' The narrator does not explain how this youthful idealism dropped away; the reader is left to infer that time and experience mean that the painter discovers that this belief cannot be sustained. He finds himself led, 'older, wiser', as the poem moves to the next stanza, drawn to depict 'more homely rooms'. Earthly accessories like pots and beds crop up; but the gold has now moved into the hangings, and the angel's wings and robes still have gorgeous touches. The use of the bracket at the beginning of the fourth verse implies the way in which our eyes can be deflected to the fashionable incidentals of the scene, rather than the undepictable mystery that is at the heart of it.

As we reach the mid-point of the poem, there is a theological statement that seems to explain this shifting painterly practice. The narrator suggests that the painter has a sense 'that his God had withdrawn'. However, this very sense is described as 'spacious', which is a generous word. It does not seem to describe a loss of faith, but perhaps a conviction that the *via negativa* is a more appropriate form of devotion; religious truth is better conveyed by envisaging less in the way of things, and more in the way of sacred space. Further paintings are made, with less detail included, though what there is has an observable reality: he 'let wall be wall', and noted the fine details of garden plants or weeds on the angel's side of the picture as he enters from the outside.

Another crucial continuation across the line break moves us into the penultimate verse. The painter is drawn 'to nothing', the sheer depiction of mysterious space, 'shadows', 'hidden rooms' that are only hinted at rather than lavishly decorated. And this finally is the point where the poem turns from gazing at an astonishingly elaborately clad angel to Mary herself, and her reaction to the news he brings. After such a smoothly described set of alternative religious scenes, the word 'shattered' strikes powerfully, suggesting the visceral human emotion evoked by such an earth-changing event. But her open consent, even to such news, is conveyed in visual form, as if she is suddenly at one with the will of the painter, as with the will of God. The narrator speaks of 'her collapsing planes/ easy and vacant'. If the heart of God is best depicted through space and nothingness, vacancy is a virtue that mirrors this. In this late painting, the angel is finally shown kneeling. It is as if Mary's reaction has brought about his stance. Instead of an artificial being encrusted with gold, he is a 'plain angel' capable of the ordinary human emotion of gratitude to a human being.

When you consider your own developing image of God over your lifetime, can you see a consistent direction of change?

18 December

The Annunciation

The angel and the girl are met.
Earth was the only meeting place.
For the embodied never yet
Travelled beyond the shore of space.
The eternal spirits in freedom go.

See, they have come together, see,
While the destroying minutes flow,
Each reflects the other's face
Till heaven in hers and earth in his
Shine steady there. He's come to her
From far beyond the farthest star,
Feathered through time. Immediacy
Of strangest strangeness is the bliss
That from their limbs all movement takes.
Yet the increasing rapture brings
So great a wonder that it makes
Each feather tremble on his wings.

Outside the window footsteps fall
Into the ordinary day
And with the sun along the wall
Pursue their unreturning way.
Sound's perpetual roundabout
Rolls its numbered octaves out
And hoarsely grinds its battered tune.

'The angel and the girl are met'

But through the endless afternoon
These neither speak nor movement make,
But stare into their deepening trance
As if their gaze would never break.

Edwin Muir

This poem by the Orcadian poet Edwin Muir asks us to gaze intently at the moment of the annunciation; it captures our focus in the same way that it seeks to depict that of the participants. It addresses the stillness and holiness of an astonishing moment when a divine messenger brings the news that heaven and earth are to be united in the body of an ordinary woman. It is a moment depicted by countless artists over the centuries, and I think it is helpful to have some of these in mind, especially medieval and renaissance paintings, when reflecting on the poem.

Although this meeting between the angel and Mary is shown in a variety of ways, there are often some common features. The picture is usually very balanced in its composition. The figures are given equal centrality, occupying their space on either side of the scene, whether standing, sitting (Mary) or kneeling (often the angel). This reflects the equal meeting of earth and heaven, but the artist frequently introduces some device to suggest a divide – maybe a pot of lilies between them, or a pillar that divides the scene. Sometimes Mary is shown turning away from the angel with apparent reluctance or puzzlement ('How shall this be?' – Luke 1.34), but more often she is facing towards the angel, with arms crossed over her chest and her eyes piously cast down in the moment of her consent. The angel always looks directly at her, and in some images she gazes back at him. Hints of heaven are shown in the earthly setting: gold leaf lights up Mary's halo, her clothes or the curtain fabrics, just as it shines from the angel's wings. There are suggestions of the interpenetration of the earthly with the divine, because this is about the mystery of the Incarnation.

The moment of consent is the tradition that Muir is drawing on in his poem, and the simple opening assertion, 'The angel and the girl are met', brings us right there, the word 'girl' highlighting Mary's youth and ordinariness. She is real and human, not a statue or some feminine ideal. The first stanza simply states the event and grounds it on earth, while announcing it as a connection between the 'embodied' girl, like all of us confined to the shores of space, and the angel in his freedom as one of the 'eternal spirits'. The poem proceeds, with occasional significant pauses between stanzas, with a smoothness and flow that echoes the extraordinary and blissful stasis at its centre. There is almost never a pause at a line ending, but there are end rhymes that recur and echo each other, without ever becoming a completely regular scheme.

The second stanza is remarkable. It starts by reminding us that we are present like worshippers at this holy and unique moment: 'See, they have come together, see'. The language here, like the word 'embodied' and the later descriptions of bliss and limbs and trembling, keeps hinting at the importance of the body in this religious moment. It is not about an achievement of enlightenment or of escaping from the boundaries of flesh and time (the next line, with its 'destroying minutes', does not let us forget the passage of time and the march of mortality). This is about an actual conception, in the body of a woman, of someone who united the human and the divine.

The narrator focuses on the two faces, their mutual gaze and the sense that they increasingly reflect each other. (Artistic depictions often show the angel and Mary with quite similar faces.) The steady absorption of their gaze is mirrored by the complete stillness of their limbs, as they experience the 'Immediacy/ Of strangest strangeness' which is the moment of Mary's consent. There is a kind of erotic tension in this description; one is reminded of John Donne's poem 'The Extasie', where the entwined lovers hold each other's gaze endlessly and time becomes eternity. The focus on the physicality of the angel's feathers paradoxically emphasizes his non-earthly reality. They have brought him 'From far beyond the farthest star,/ Feathered through time' (hear the wing beats suggested by the alliteration here), and it is in his feathers that he shivers with awe.

There is a pause and we are suddenly made aware of the prosaic sounds of everyday life going on outside Mary's window in the 'ordinary day'. There are footsteps that do not return (as the events of this holy moment set in train some consequences that cannot now be recalled), and the 'perpetual roundabout' of sounds, like a hoarse and melancholy organ grinder with its 'battered tune'. This is the depressing context in which salvation, engendered here, will have to operate. Then the poem returns to the holy, still atmosphere of that 'endless afternoon', a phrase that in two words unites earth and heaven. It is a boundaried span of time between noon and sunset, and yet it is a piece of eternity.

Have you ever experienced a sense of religious awe? What happened, and what difference has it made to your life?

19 December

The Visitation

She had not held her secret long enough
To covet it but wished it shared as though
Telling would tame the terrifying moment
When she, most calm in her own afternoon,
    Felt the intrepid angel, heard
His beating wings, his voice across her prayer.

This was the thing she needed to impart,
The uncalm moment, the strange interruption,
The angel bringing pain disguised as joy,
But mixed with this was something she could share
    And not abandon, simply how
A child sprang in her like the first of seeds.

And in the stillness of that other day
The afternoon exposed its emptiness,
Shadows adrift from light, the long road turning
In a dry sequence of the sun. And she
    No apprehensive figure seemed,
Only a moving silence through the land.

And all her journeying was a caressing
Within her mind of secrets to be spoken.
The simple fact of birth soon overshadowed
The shadow of the angel. When she came
    Close to her cousin's house she kept
Only the message of her happiness.

And those two women in their quick embrace
Gazed at each other with looks undisturbed
By men or miracles. It was the child
Who laid his shadow on their afternoon
    By stirring suddenly, by bringing
Back the broad echoes of those beating wings.

Elizabeth Jennings

Like the poets above, Elizabeth Jennings also engaged in some extended poetic meditation on the story of what happened to Mary. She wrote a sequence of two poems about the aftermath of the angelic annunciation: one that imagines Mary's response moments after the angel has departed, and this one, about Mary's visit to her cousin Elizabeth. Luke's Gospel frames the story of Jesus' conception and birth within the story of his cousin John the Baptist's conception and birth (Luke 1—2). Elizabeth's conception of John is a miraculous one too, since she was past the age of childbearing, and she conceals her pregnancy for about five months. It is then, in the 'sixth month' of Elizabeth's pregnancy, that the angel appears to Mary, and after the encounter Mary immediately sets out to visit her cousin. The greeting between the two pregnant women is famously celebrated by Elizabeth's awareness that her baby 'leaped in her womb' when Mary's voice was heard. Luke may have understood this to be the 'quickening' of John, but in any case the biblical account here is deeply joyful, and has become the source for important elements of Christian liturgy, such as the 'Hail Mary!' and the Magnificat.

Jennings' poem has a rather different feel. It takes as its cue the troubled reaction of Mary to the presence of the angel (Luke 1.29), and traces through, entering into Mary's thought processes as she visits her cousin, an ambivalence about what she has taken on. It becomes a meditation on the difficulty of sharing a profound and deeply private religious experience, and on how responding to the divine call is never going to be solely a matter of unalloyed joy.

Like Muir's poem, this one focuses on key moments that happen during afternoons: the angel's interruption of Mary's calm devotions is recalled as happening 'in her own afternoon'; Mary is seen travelling during another afternoon which 'exposed its emptiness' in the hot sun; Mary and Elizabeth have 'their afternoon' of greeting and embrace. So the first stanza is a looking back to the moment of the angel's arrival, seen through the prism of Mary's sense of holding an immense and awesome secret. The narrator assumes that the reader knows the story and understands what the secret is, with all its implications of immediate shame and future hardship and heartache. Mary is full of the secret, overwhelmed by it, not wanting to 'covet' or possess it for herself but rather to alleviate her fear by telling someone 'as though/ Telling would tame the terrifying moment'. Notice the alliteration, which makes the line sound urgent, like someone letting out information suddenly and forcefully. Like much of Christian tradition, Jennings imagines Mary at prayer when the angel arrives. But there is a sense that this is someone who intended her prayer to be 'most calm' and to remain that way. She did not foresee that the divine presence might be 'intrepid', or involve 'beating wings', or terror.

The second stanza explores the contrast between the unexpectedly troubling presence of the angel and the simple delight in knowing that she has conceived a child, who 'sprang in her like the first of seeds'. There is an interesting tension between what 'she needed to impart' and the 'something she could share'. What she cannot articulate is 'The uncalm moment, the strange interruption,/ The angel bringing pain disguised as joy'. God's choice of her, a devout woman, has turned what was calm into the 'uncalm'; has interrupted her prayer with his presence; has apparently offered joy, but wrapped within that comes certain pain. This predictable pain is witnessed to in the biblical account. After Jesus' birth, when he is brought to be presented in the Temple, the old man Simeon recognizes the child for who he is, and says to Mary: 'A sword will pierce through your own soul also' (Luke 2.35). Nevertheless, in this poem it is as if Mary gradually foregrounds the joy in her heart and lets the secret fear withdraw.

The poem gives the whole of the next stanza to Mary's journey, almost as if to allow some narrative time between the recollection of the annunciation and Mary's arrival in the hill country where

Elizabeth lives. Although it is about travel, there is a curious sense of stasis about the afternoon; it is a sort of limbo period. It has 'stillness' and 'emptiness'. Mary herself is described, as if from a distance, as 'Only a moving silence'. The narrator mentions 'Shadows adrift from light', conveying both a hot, windless afternoon but also a period when the 'shadows' that are Mary's fears seem to come gently apart from the 'light' that is her sense of joy. So by the time the next stanza begins, she has become someone who is preoccupied in a delighted way about her 'secrets to be spoken'. The term 'caressing' is beautiful, suggesting the expectation of tending lovingly to the child who is the burden of her secret. The excitement overcomes her fear: 'The simple fact of birth soon overshadowed/ The shadow of the angel'. The repetition of 'shadow' (which is included in the word 'overshadow') models how anxiety has been encompassed by joyful expectation. Mary resolves only to share 'the message of her happiness'.

It is only in the final stanza that the 'visitation' of the poem's title is achieved – all the rest of it has been about the journey and planning of what to share. The 'gaze' between the two women in their 'quick embrace' is an interesting contrast with the endless gaze of the girl and the angel described by Muir. It is refreshingly down to earth – the connection between two related women as they share the fact of each other's pregnancy 'undisturbed/ By men or miracles'. Yoking 'men' and 'miracles' in this ironic way speaks of a sort of sisterhood of women, who have to get on with the actual business of childbirth on their own, whatever the origin of the conception, human or divine. But then comes the intervention of 'the child/ Who laid his shadow on their afternoon/ By stirring suddenly'. This is presumably Elizabeth's child, but it is as if Mary herself feels it, and for her the quickening child brings back the 'broad echoes of those beating wings'. The fearfulness of the annunciation is once more where she, and we as the readers, are left.

Have you ever found that there was something about your relationship with God that has been quite impossible to communicate to anyone else?

20 December

Northumbrian Sequence, 4

Let in the wind
Let in the rain
Let in the moors tonight.

The storm beats on my window-pane,
Night stands at my bed-foot,
Let in the fear,
Let in the pain,
Let in the trees that toss and groan,
Let in the north tonight.

Let in the nameless formless power
That beats upon my door,
Let in the ice, let in the snow,
The banshee howling on the moor,
The bracken-bush on the bleak hillside,
Let in the dead tonight.

The whistling ghost behind the dyke,
The dead that rot in mire,
Let in the thronging ancestors,
The unfulfilled desire,
Let in the wraith of the dead earl,
Let in the unborn tonight.

Let in the cold,
Let in the wet,
Let in the loneliness,
Let in the quick,

Let in the dead,
Let in the unpeopled skies.

Oh how can virgin fingers weave
A covering for the void,
How can my fearful heart conceive
Gigantic solitude?
How can a house so small contain
A company so great?
Let in the dark,
Let in the dead,
Let in your love tonight.

Let in the snow that numbs the grave,
Let in the acorn-tree,
The mountain stream and mountain stone,
Let in the bitter sea.

Fearful is my virgin heart
And frail my virgin form,
And must I then take pity on
The raging of the storm
That rose up from the great abyss
Before the earth was made,
That pours the stars in cataracts
And shakes this violent world?

Let in the fire,
Let in the power,
Let in the invading might.

Gentle must my fingers be
And pitiful my heart
Since I must bind in human form
A living power so great,
A living impulse great and wild
That cries about my house
With all the violence of desire
Desiring this my peace.

Pitiful my heart must hold
The lonely stars at rest
Have pity on the raven's cry
The torrent and the eagle's wing,
The icy water of the tarn
And on the biting blast.

Let in the wound,
Let in the pain,
Let in your child tonight.

Kathleen Raine

This poem is not unequivocally about the fears of a young woman, a virgin, who has become pregnant with God's child – but it well could be; and the terrified tone of the poem represents one possible way of reacting to a growing realization of what has been set in train. The work was published in the same volume as a sequence of three poems that are explicitly about the Incarnation. In one of these, the Christ-child is addressed, in a very similar setting to this one: 'Who stands at my door in the storm and the rain/ On the threshold of being?/ One who waits till you call him in . . . I am your child.' So it is a theme that Raine was definitely exploring at the time (1952), although in both poems we may feel that the 'child' also, perhaps even primarily, refers to some key aspect of the narrator's own psyche or 'inner child'.

Certainly we are in Gothic territory (one is reminded of *Wuthering Heights*), solidly located in the robust winter weather of Northumbria, as the poem's title suggests. Although the speaker is indoors, there is throughout the poem a raw sense of the fearful world of the outdoor landscape, with its serious wind, rain and icy cold battering on an all-too-fragile door. The text is rather like a lament, a cry of terror, that deserves to be chanted out loud to get the full effect of the writing. It is deeply repetitive, with its endless imperative 'Let in . . .' addressed to all sorts of things that one would much rather not let in on such a night. It is hard not to feel chilled by the recitation.

Starting initially with simply the bleak landscape of the moors, we quickly move on to the kind of weather that seems to be demanding to be let in. Instead of the traditional angels of the old children's prayer standing at the bedside, it is the sinister 'Night', and suddenly pain and fear are included in the list, and even the trees. They 'toss and groan' (a wonderful evocation of a gale-force wind), rather as the narrator is probably doing in her own troubled bed. The next two stanzas definitely inhabit the realm of nightmare and perhaps local spooky legends: a 'nameless formless power', the 'banshee howling', the 'whistling ghost', the 'thronging ancestors', the 'unborn', and, repeatedly, 'the dead'.

In the fifth stanza, the lines are shorter, simpler and less hysterical, and I think at the heart of them is the line 'Let in the loneliness'; this, along with the later 'Let in your love tonight', may be the underlying cause for the sense of panic in the poem. This is further explored in the next verse, where it is plausible that the speaker is indeed Mary rehearsing her fears about her body, the conception itself, her isolation, her terror at having her body house 'a company so great'. Then she is back to the familiar form of the refrain, before asserting plainly her own fragility, not just in the face of northern weather, but, it is suggested, the apocalyptic events that have rocked the universe and made her conception a necessity. For the storm and the 'great abyss/ Before the earth was made' may be referring to the fallen angels and the opening up of the pits of evil that gave rise to a 'violent world'. Or these lines may simply convey her terror at opening herself to the tremendous forces of creation itself.

If the narrator is indeed contemplating her task in giving birth to and raising the child of God, there is nothing whatever soft or sentimental about the prospect. She calls her fingers 'gentle' and her heart 'pitiful' (full of pity? pitiably inadequate?); but they are all she has with which to bind 'in human form/ A living power so great . . . and wild'. She sees this power as violent in its desires, crying about her house and at the doors of her heart and likely to take away all her peace of mind. Yet as the agonized lament comes to its close, there is a growing sense of acceptance of the role she must take on. It is as if her consent gives her the power to encompass and even to 'have pity' on the rigours of the landscape. And this is mirrored by her capacity to take on, as indeed God will do in taking flesh, the irreversible 'wound' of love: 'Let in your child tonight.'

Is there anything that you are afraid of, but must face?

21 December

At the Winter Solstice

The pines look black in the half-
light of dawn. Stillness . . .
While we slept an inch of new snow
simplified the field. Today of all days
the sun will shine no more
than is strictly necessary.

At the village church last night
the boys – shepherds and wisemen –
pressed close to the manger in obedience,
wishing only for time to pass;
but the girl dressed as Mary trembled
as she leaned over the pungent hay,
and like the mother of Christ
wondered why she had been chosen.

After the pageant, a ruckus of cards,
presents, and homemade Christmas sweets.
A few of us stayed to clear the bright
scraps and ribbons from the pews,
and lift the pulpit back in place.

When I opened the hundred-year-old Bible
to Luke's account of the Epiphany
black dust from the binding rubbed off
on my hands, and on the altar cloth.

Jane Kenyon

We have reached the season of nativity plays, these days always enacted by children and watched, with poignant feelings, by the adults to whom they are attached, whether or not those parents still subscribe to a belief in the events portrayed. This poem by Jane Kenyon focuses on one such sweet occasion, set at the time of the winter solstice, the darkest day of the year in the northern hemisphere. Although the poet leaves the reader a great deal of the work of interpretation to do, what's clear is that underlying the innocent festive event are some troubling layers. It is not just about what the adults know, namely that all of life isn't like a magical nativity play: rather, the story itself has the power to set off troubling thoughts.

With four stanzas of varying lengths and no end rhymes, it reads like a conversational 'debriefing' set of thoughts about the nativity play that happened the previous evening. It begins with the look of the landscape as day dawns – very late, and rather faintly. At one level, the choice of observation is casual: 'The pines look black' against the dawn light and the new snow. But, as we shall see, things that are black, and their impact on whiteness, will recur at the end of the poem as well. Without spelling it out, there is an implied opposition between light and dark going on, or at least a suggestion that the two are mingled in a disconcerting and unexpected way. The next observation is about the new snowfall, which occurred during sleep, and the word 'simplified' is brilliant. It is not easy to find an unclichéd way of describing the transformation of a landscape made by untouched snow. This single word instantly evokes that brilliant ironing out of bumps and lumps, which draws the whole view together in an impression of unity. The final remark is about the daylight, pointing out that it will be minimal: 'no more/ than is strictly necessary' almost suggests cosmic efficiency policies, or an austerity that has a purpose. Necessary for what? Continued life? Or for humans to grasp the point of something on this crucial 'hinge' day, after which the light starts to return?

Then the narrator starts to outline what happened at the nativity play. There is a contrast between the boys, who did what they were told but were apparently untouched by the story or their various roles in it, and 'the girl dressed as Mary' who was carrying the central role. She depicts this contrast by close attention to small details of their demeanour. The boys 'pressed close to the manger in obedience' (notice the way the cluster of sibilant consonants implies a crush of bodies). They are, she infers, concerned with ordinary time and impatient to get the performance over with. The girl with the central role seems to be affected by the mystery. Again there are just some key arresting details. She 'trembled/ as she leaned over the pungent hay'. This beautifully captures the child's shiver of awe, the attention to the Christchild, and the reality of the fragrant hay (this is a rural context and the real material is available). Notice that the 'baby' – presumably a doll here – is not actually described. But the scent of the hay makes him feel mysteriously present. It is well known that the role of Mary is hotly competed for, but there may be mixed feelings in the chosen girl: is it because she is beautiful, or biddable, or good at performing – or perhaps she is genuinely special and the fact that she has been chosen is something that will affect her life? The poem places the child in direct descent to the accounts of Mary, which show her troubled about why she has been chosen (Luke 1.29).

The third stanza is back in the world of ordinary reality: the aftermath of the play, the exchange of cards ('ruckus' suggests a happy sort of chaos of meeting and greeting), and then the clear-up after the crowds have thinned. There is a bright innocence about the colourful scraps of homemade Christmas decorations that have been used to deck the church. And the pulpit, which is clearly a movable item, needs putting back in place.

The final verse is full of puzzles which are not resolved. Part of the task of restoring the pulpit and its contents to its normal place is handling the large pulpit Bible, more than a century old. This needs to be opened at the place where the next reader of the lesson in church will want it. Most churches have a large Bible for reading out loud, and if they have not got round to purchasing a modern version (or perhaps can't afford it) this is likely to be a vast leather-bound tome with the old language that has been used for generations. The narrator speaks of trying to find 'Luke's account of the Epiphany', which is very odd, since Luke doesn't give an account of the Epiphany, the visit of the magi; this story occurs only in Matthew. With a writer who chooses her words as carefully as Kenyon, it seems unlikely that this is an unintentional error. She could equally well have used the term 'nativity' (it would have fitted), but perhaps she is suggesting the next stage of the narrative. Of course, the magi themselves looked in the wrong place first; perhaps we all do.

And then there is the detail of the black dust from the ageing leather binding, which gets onto the narrator's hands 'and on the altar cloth' (the pure white cloth always laid on top of whatever other cloth adorns the altar). What does this detail mean, apart from the fact that it happened and, given the age of the item, is not surprising? Some might interpret the elderly Bible as symbolizing traditional churchgoing and its sense of decay. But the poem has precisely pinpointed how the re-enactment of a half-believed story has the power to excite a local community and to affect a child with the serious and unsettling truth of what it is about. In the same way, this adult, having watched the events and then been community-minded enough to help clear up, has found that these precise actions have got her hands dirty and made her notice how light and darkness are mingled. This is not a million miles from grasping what incarnation is about.

Notice your reactions to the various Christmas events in your own church. What particularly touches you about them?

22 December

————•◦•————

Ode to Winter

We hoard light, hunkered in holt and burrow,
in cave, *cwtsh*, den, earth, hut, lair.
Sun blinks. Trees take down their hair.
Dusk wipes horizons, seeps into the room,
the last flame of geranium in the gloom.

In the shortening day, bring in the late flowers
to crisp in a vase, beech to break into leaf,
a branch of larch. Take winter by the throat.
Feed the common birds, tits and finches,
the spotted woodpecker in his opera coat.

Let's learn to love the icy winter moon,
or moonless dark and winter constellations,
Jupiter's glow, a slow, incoming plane,
neighbourly windows, someone's flickering screen,
a lamp-lit page, drawn curtains.

Let us praise intimacy, talk and books,
music and silence, wind and rain,
the beautiful bones of trees, taste of cold air,
darkening fields, the glittering city,
that winter longing, *hiraeth*, something like prayer.

Under the stilled heartbeat of trees,
wind-snapped branches, mulch and root,
a million bluebell bulbs lie low
ready to flare in lengthening light,
after the dark, the frozen earth, the snow.

Out there, fox and buzzard, kite and crow
are clearing the ground for the myth.
On the darkest day bring in the tree,
cool and pungent as forest. Turn up the music.
Pour us a glass. Dress the house in pagan finery.

Gillian Clarke

Like the previous poem, this one is set on the day with the least amount of daylight, but the focus here is the efforts of human beings as we try to deal with the dead of winter, the cold, the lack of light. Each year there is a flurry of activity; some of it is to do straightforwardly with keeping warm and safe, but much is about celebration, and about enjoying what deep winter can be about, both indoors and out. There are six five-line stanzas, with occasional end rhymes but nothing regular. It is called an 'ode' and it is indeed a praise poem, a kind of toast to the possibilities of a season when so many things have shut down or become dormant.

It starts with the battle to 'hoard light', which is scarce and therefore precious at this time. The alliteration leads us into the long list of words, basically all describing a cosy bolt-hole, for which we yearn, 'hunkered' against the chill. '*Cwtsh*' is a snug Welsh word that can be used for any small protected space, like a cupboard, a hut or a coal-hole, but can also refer to a hug. 'Trees take down their hair' is an unusual way of describing the leaf fall, and stands in marked contrast with some of the other images explored in this book (see Rowan Williams' image of flaying on p. 1). Clarke's words prepare for the poem's invitation to party at the end. Then there is the image of the dusk wiping horizons, almost like someone wiping the surfaces in a room that is being prepared for a particular purpose. The outdoor seems to come indoors here; the orange sunset, 'the last flame of geranium', mirrors the final petals of the tender pot plant that has been brought indoors to flower as late as possible.

The second stanza picks up the same idea, about bringing plants inside either to last longer or to force their buds in the warmth, and the narrator describes this human habit at this time of year in a very forceful way: 'Take winter by the throat'. The same impulse to vanquish the effects of cold is seen in our feeding of the birds, both common and rare. The 'spotted woodpecker in his opera coat' not only highlights the dramatic and showy markings of that bird but once again contributes to the dressed-up winter party atmosphere.

The next two verses complement each other; the first starts outdoors and gradually moves towards the warmth of the home, the next begins indoors but gives a strong sense of being surrounded by wintry beauty without. In both we are enjoined to learn to love and praise the glories of this time of year. The cosmic landscape of the sky gives place to human constructions (the 'slow, incoming plane') and the cosy glimpse through half-drawn curtains of the neighbourly life within. So there is a list of what should be enjoyed, which mingles the inner and the outer; intimacy, books and talk give way to wind, rain, 'the beautiful bones of trees' (not at all sinister here) and the 'glittering city' lit up in the early twilight. All these contribute to a definition of what I think this poem is all about: 'that winter longing, *hiraeth*, something like prayer'. For although the theme is in some ways frankly pagan, this yearning is the heart of it, and it is like prayer. While '*hiraeth*' is untranslatable, it is a word specific to a deep longing for Wales, and so describes the pull that draws one home. We are back longing for our *cwtsh*.

The penultimate verse bears witness to what cannot be seen outdoors, but we know exists, 'Under the stilled heartbeat of trees' (but dormant, not really dead, ready to rise) – the electrifying 'million bluebell bulbs' that will respond to the lengthening light when this time of deadness is past. The word 'flare' in relation to flowers refers us back to 'the last flame of geranium', and the promise of the next growing season follows hard on the heels of the demise of the last. This wintry cold actually houses a landscape ready to explode with life at any moment.

Finally, the narrator envisages the predators who are still hunting in the dark, preparing for the 'myth', the mystery of the coming of the light. We humans are invited to participate in hope of the light's return by bringing in the Christmas tree, dressing it in 'pagan finery', and joining the party.

What do you most enjoy about indoor celebrations around this time of year? Which traditions are important to you?

23 December

seasonal *ghazal*

the silent stars descend to us
come angel seraph sheep pear-tree

o holy o cold
dawn come in snow

offspring of day
light is lily above us

glory birds, calling birds
sun, the fields shining

the day, the earth, skies
peace, contemplation and music

hosanna, no, holly stand
suddenly tree displayed

the yonder star our comfort
bring time again

joy, *excelsis* a-leaping
world and hope embrace

lullay image and sing sing
a happy new begin

Harry Gilonis

The '*ghazal*' in this poem's title is an ancient form of Arabic verse
dating from the sixth century, composed and sung widely in the
Arabic-speaking world, in Turkey and various Indian languages. Its

traditional form has as many constraints as the classic Petrarchan sonnet: it typically consists of five or more couplets, all of which share the same metre, though the theme of each couplet may not be closely linked to the others. It is the poetic expression of the pain of loss or separation, shot through with a sense of beauty, and its normal theme is unattainable love. Frequently, the Beloved becomes a metaphor for God, and so the poetry is melancholy, full of love and longing and metaphysical questions. Such diverse poets as Rumi in the thirteenth century and Ghalib and Goethe in the nineteenth century have used the form.

Poets writing in English tend to use the form in a looser fashion, and this poem by Harry Gilonis is an example of this. It is also quite experimental in that it eschews punctuation and capitalization, and the grammar is deliberately chaotic. Although it is divided into couplets, overall it gives the impression of a medley of glowing fragments of meaning that have been brought together in a way that, strangely, does convey an intense seasonal yearning.

One of the extraordinary but completely familiar features of the way we celebrate Christmas, the coming of the Christian saviour, is how we mix our traditions, blending Christian carols and readings with pagan songs and practices and finding no discontinuity there. This poem gives an impression of naivety but in fact skilfully works with tiny facets of memory or tradition to reflect this blend. Is the first line a description of the mystery, or is it an invocation to the stars to come to earth? It is composed of two snatches from the carol 'O little town of Bethlehem': in the first verse the sleeping town is envisaged, as 'the silent stars go by'; in the last verse we invoke the holy child of Bethlehem, 'descend to us, we pray'. So the whole carol and its prayer is the reference in just one line. The second line of that couplet lists a mixture of creatures, from angels to pear-trees; we are whisking through the biblical narratives of the nativity, and including for good measure the pear-tree which has a partridge in it, in the traditional song 'The Twelve Days of Christmas'.

Each of the subsequent couplets could be mined for similar references, possibly double or triple references. 'O holy' could mean the child of Bethlehem or the 'holy night' of the carol 'Silent Night'.

The 'snow' might be from Christina Rossetti's poem that begins 'In the bleak mid-winter' (p. 94) – or any number of other carols. The 'offspring of day' could be a reference to Jesus as the Son of God, but also to the 'dayspring from on high' of which the Benedictus speaks (Luke 1.78). The words 'light is lily above us' stunningly evoke the illumination of the skies when the angelic host sang 'Glory to God in the highest' to the shepherds. Or they could be referencing other mentions of lilies, such as in the Song of Songs (2.1–2), that classic love poem that has been interpreted (like many ghazals) as witnessing to the yearning of the soul for God. And, of course, lilies are associated with the Virgin Mary.

But then again, 'The Twelve Days of Christmas' (itself a song about 'my true love') emerge again in the 'calling birds', which are rather like singing angels, though they come from a quite different strand of tradition. The praise seems to encompass all that is – the day, the earth, the skies – with the Gloria's promise of peace. Suddenly, though, the 'hosanna' morphs into 'holly' (perhaps from 'The Holly and the Ivy') and the Christmas tree displayed with decorations. Then the sequence buckles back again to 'yonder star' that guided the magi – that classic journey of longing that followed an implausible phenomenon to an improbable and humble place. There is the promise of 'comfort', and then 'joy', echoing 'God Rest Ye Merry' with its refrain bringing 'comfort and joy'.

Then, *'excelsis'* (Latin for 'the highest', a snatch of the angel's Gloria) is juxtaposed with 'a-leaping' (like the 'twelve lords'). The world and hope embrace, and the final couplet bids us sing with a hint of the Coventry Carol ('Lully lullay'). The end suggests a happy new beginning, but the grammar denies us this expectation. Instead, the verb is imperative: 'begin'. The excited, uplifted yearning of this little poem that draws on so much tells us actively to get started on the celebration, and on the change it brings.

What are the connections or tensions for you between Christian beliefs and the traditional pagan practices around Christmas/Yuletide?

24 December

In the Days of Caesar

In the days of Caesar, when his subjects went to be reckoned,
there was a poem made, too dark for him (naive with power)
     to read.
It was a bunch of shepherds who discovered
in Bethlehem of Judah, the great music beyond reason and
     reckoning:
shepherds, the sort of folk who leave the ninety-nine behind
so as to bring the stray back home, they heard it clear,
the subtle assonances of the day, dawning toward cock-crow,
the birthday of the Lamb of God, shepherd of mortals.

Well, little people, and my little nation, can you see
the secret buried in you, that no Caesar ever captures in his lists?
Will not the shepherd come to fetch us in our desert,
gathering us in to give us birth again, weaving us into one
in a song heard in the sky over Bethlehem?
He seeks us out as wordhoard for his workmanship, the laureate
     of heaven.

Waldo Williams, translated from the Welsh by Rowan Williams

Waldo Williams was one of the foremost poets writing in Welsh in the twentieth century, a Baptist who was very active in politics. He was a Welsh nationalist, a pacifist and an anti-war campaigner, and was involved in a sustained protest against the Korean War, withholding his income tax and spending time in prison as a result. He continued his protest until the ending of compulsory National Service in 1963, and subsequently protested against military installations in

Wales. This poem is addressed to the people of Wales, comparing them with the lowly shepherds who were shown the glory of heaven and summoned to the stable on the night of Christ's birth. It is set 'In the days of Caesar' (which is also how Luke begins his account of the nativity), and the reader is very conscious of implicit correspondences between the Jewish people, occupied by the power of Rome, and the 'little people' of Wales in the context of British power.

The poem is a sonnet, with the traditional contrast between the first eight lines (focusing on the shepherds then) and the final six (addressing the Welsh people now). In this translation by Rowan Williams, the lines are lengthy and not completely regular, and the language is an interesting mixture of the colloquial ('It was a bunch of shepherds'), the literary critical ('the subtle assonances of the day') and the archaic ('wordhoard for his workmanship'). The last phrase reflects the alliteration that is typical of Welsh poetry. There is a challenge to the people of Wales to believe in themselves, but the tone is tender rather than campaigning, and because of the identification with the shepherds of Bethlehem, it is easy to read this poem as relevant to all those whom the Bible calls 'little ones' or 'babes', who are seen as unimportant by the powers that be (Matthew 11.25), and yet have been granted insight hidden from these.

There is another controlling metaphor within the poem, that of poetry itself, unfolding the central mystery of the Incarnation. The event that the shepherds were called to witness is explained thus: 'there was a poem made . . . the great music beyond reason and reckoning' (note that the subjects of Caesar went to be 'reckoned'). This 'poem' was something that Caesar was unable to understand. It was 'too dark for him (naive with power) to read'. Here, using the word 'dark' instead of 'difficult' suggests something that is out of sight. The phrase 'naive with power' is fascinating. 'Naive' normally applies to someone who is inexperienced in the ways of the world, and therefore unlikely to be effective in it, indeed appearing silly and immature. It is not normally attached to those who wield power. And yet the bracketed aside jolts the reader with its insight. Of course those who have achieved political power or wealth do not see clearly many of the realities that the 'little people' experience every day. And just as Augustus Caesar was completely oblivious to the significance of what was going on at Bethlehem in his era, so 'the secret buried in you' (the Welsh people) is something that no modern equivalent of Caesar 'ever catches in his lists'.

What is distinctive about the shepherds, and why did they hear the music of this great poem? Notice that the poet does not spell out the story of the angelic choir in the sky; rather, the emphasis is on the acute hearing of the shepherds themselves ('they heard it clear'). The dawning of the new day is an implicit image of the coming of the light in Christ. The shepherds, it is suggested, had this ability to grasp the mystery because they were 'the sort of folk who leave the ninety-nine behind/ so as to bring the stray back home'. Thus the parable of the good shepherd, which Jesus will later tell, is introduced as something inspired by people like these shepherds; and their key quality is to seek out the forgotten and the unimportant – against all sensible cost-efficiency strategies. In this they reflect the impossibly generous nature of the God who became human in the stable, who seeks out the humble and dwells with them. The last line of the octet hammers home how many images taken from the shepherd's own world have been claimed for the child of Bethlehem: the 'Lamb of God, shepherd of mortals' (see John 1.29).

The final sestet offers hope to the Welsh people, and all little ones, that this shepherd will seek us out, 'fetch us in our desert' and weave us into the same song that was 'heard in the sky over Bethlehem'. This song, we remember, was not only about glory to God but also about peace to all people, when there will be no need for campaigning against war and oppression, and the Word of God will be heard even by the world's Caesars. But I think it also suggests that the little people, who heard the song before the powerful did, have a part to play in bringing about such an event. The beautiful last line contains an image of God as poet, searching among us who are his precious and abundant 'wordhoard' to create a poem for today: 'He seeks us out as wordhoard for his workmanship, the laureate of heaven.' As we celebrate the Word made flesh, this poem speaks of how humans are 'spoken' by God.

As you prepare to attend Christmas worship, use this poem to reflect on the mystery of the Incarnation.

25 December

BC:AD

This was the moment when Before
Turned into After, and the future's
Uninvented timekeepers presented arms.

This was the moment when nothing
Happened. Only dull peace
Sprawled boringly over the earth.

This was the moment when even energetic Romans
Could find nothing better to do
Than counting heads in remote provinces.

And this was the moment
When a few farm workers and three
Members of an obscure Persian sect

Walked haphazard by starlight straight
Into the kingdom of heaven.

U. A. Fanthorpe

U. A. Fanthorpe, a Quaker, used to write a new Christmas poem
each year, to include with Christmas cards to her friends. These are
always short, and seek for a fresh and unsentimental take on the
familiar story; along with an often comic approach there is always
that authentic jolt for the reader, which reminds us of the extraor-
dinary nature of the gospel truth.

This poem is in the form of a Shakespearean sonnet, but the lines
are divided into threes rather than fours, each one beginning with
the phrase 'This was the moment . . .' The climax certainly comes

in the last couplet, but instead of standing alone it is set up by the fourth triplet. This seems as informal and inconsequential as the earlier part of the poem, but its meandering 'ho-hum' tone is suddenly interrupted by a surprisingly forceful theological punchline in the last two.

The poem starts by playing with the concept of 'BC' (Before Christ) turning into 'AD' (Anno Domini, the year of our Lord). This is a fascinating thought for the nerdy child in all of us (I cannot be alone in having wondered about it in my youth), although as adults we know that this way of dividing historical time was established much later – probably post-Constantine. And indeed, astronomical and other evidence suggests that the birth of Jesus – certainly a historical figure – probably happened a few years earlier than the date when BC and AD notionally changed places. The poem shows its awareness of all this by comically having 'the future's/ Uninvented timekeepers' present arms. It makes me think of those absurd mechanical clocks seen on some town halls, when pompous little figures pop out from each side on the stroke of the hour and salute each other.

The second triplet arrestingly asserts that 'This was the moment when nothing/ Happened.' Given that we have been preparing ourselves to greet an event that faith sees as the most significant event in history, is this not blasphemous? Well, it is important to look carefully at where the emphasis on those two words 'nothing' and 'Happened' should be placed. They are divided by the line break quite deliberately, and the reader is led to give weight to the word 'Happened'. Perhaps something important did happen, and a good way of describing that is to name it 'nothing'. The poem immediately defines one kind of the 'nothing' that is meant, pointing out that 'peace on earth' (announced by the angels) is at one level a blessed absence of conflict and war. The narrator describes it almost as if Peace is a soporific relative visiting for Christmas and currently slumped on the sofa; so again, we are denied any sentimental thoughts about peace, while having to admit the accuracy of what it might mean. Sadly, human beings seem to see lack of conflict as rather 'dull', and look for ways to get passionate in fighting each other or testing out expensive new weapons we have developed.

There may be another way of thinking about the 'nothing' that nevertheless 'Happened'. Other poems in this selection explore the significance of 'absence' as possessing a curious power and reality in the divine economy and our human grasp of this (see 'The Absence' by R. S. Thomas, p. 28; or Gwyneth Lewis' 'Annunciation' from her sequence 'Six Poems about Nothing', p. 62). In the same way that technically the change from BC to AD would give you a year zero, perhaps this nothing out of the ordinary is nevertheless a world-changing 'nothing'. It is the spiritual practice of Quakers to meet in order to sit in silence together; and it is at the heart of their belief that this is precisely the silence into which the Spirit can be heard to speak.

The third 'this was the moment' highlights the role in the story of the Roman occupiers of Palestine at the time of Christ. The 'dull' theme is pursued again, and the emphasis is on tedious administration rather than glamorous conquest or tyrannical cruelty towards the conquered. The historical moment that brought Mary and Joseph to Bethlehem in the first place was a census. We are told about this in language that is remote from the way the Bible tells the story; instead of appearing to describe the context for a mystery, the events are presented from the perspective of Rome, which certainly did not perceive Judea as the centre of the universe. It is just a matter of 'counting heads in remote provinces'.

The final triplet continues to describe the players in the story with a tone of boredom, and it is refreshing to hear the familiar shepherds referred to as 'a few farm workers' and the magi as 'three/ Members of an obscure Persian sect'. It removes from them their revered status as well-loved figures in a nativity scene, and makes us realize that we would pay no such devout attention to these players if we met them in their contemporary equivalents. This actually brings home the impact of the initial birth narratives: shepherds were low-status 'unclean' people, unable because of their work to fulfil all the requirements of the Law, while travelling foreigners with bizarre beliefs, however learned, were no doubt thought to be as odd then as they would be today.

And then comes the final couplet, which conveys a sudden end to the meandering style, just as it presents the astonishment of the

participants at the place they have ended up. Nothing out of the or-
dinary happened: a human child was born in humble circumstances
like many before him and since. And yet at the same time the place
they walked into 'haphazard by starlight' was simultaneously no less
than 'the kingdom of heaven'. We can end up there too.

Find time to write your own brief Christmas poem.

26 December

A Christmas Carol

In the bleak mid-winter
    Frosty wind made moan,
Earth stood hard as iron,
    Water like a stone;
Snow had fallen, snow on snow,
    Snow on snow,
In the bleak mid-winter
    Long ago.

Our God, Heaven cannot hold Him
    Nor earth sustain;
Heaven and earth shall flee away
    When he comes to reign:
In the bleak mid-winter
    A stable-place sufficed
The Lord God Almighty
    Jesus Christ.

Enough for Him, whom cherubim
    Worship night and day,
A breastful of milk
    And a mangerful of hay;
Enough for Him, whom angels
    Fall down before,
The ox and ass and camel
    Which adore.

Angels and archangels
    May have gathered there,

Cherubim and seraphim
    Thronged the air;
But only His mother
    In her maiden bliss
Worshipped the Beloved
    With a kiss.

What can I give Him,
    Poor as I am?
If I were a shepherd
    I would bring a lamb,
If I were a Wise Man
    I would do my part, –
Yet what I can I give Him,
    Give my heart.

Christina Rossetti

'In the bleak mid-winter' has frequently been nominated as our favourite Christmas carol, but it was written initially as a Christmas poem for a literary magazine in 1874, not to be sung. It is not easy to read the poem without hearing the famous tune, composed by Gustav Holst more than 30 years after the text was written. Although it has five matching stanzas and a simple, regular end-rhyme scheme throughout, the metre is irregular by the standards of hymnody. The tune has to be flexible enough for slightly more or slightly fewer syllables to be fitted in as the lines are sung. But one of the effects of this has been to disguise the impact of the last line of each stanza, which is shorter than all the rest – a very brief two-beat line where the rhythm might lead us to expect three beats. (The classic tune converts this back to three beats.) What we have is a deceptively simple-sounding poem, which culminates at the end of each verse with a phrase that is even more spare and direct.

The short lines and the easy pattern of the rhymes make this poem sound almost like something written for children, but the underlying theology is profound, and I suspect that the simple form is a deliberate reflection on that theology, with its emphasis on God's self-emptying in the Incarnation (Philippians 2.5–9). Spareness, austerity, and utter human simplicity: these are what the maker of earth and heaven chose in taking human flesh.

The first stanza simply describes the wintry weather. Although Bethlehem can get cold and wet in the winter, this seems to be a deliberate evocation of a much more northerly winter, such as our own. The emphasis is on sheer hardship: the context was 'bleak', the wind moaning in the cold (as a baby would do), the earth arrested with frost (as in Rowan Williams' poem, p. 1), water is iced over and therefore difficult to access. Although many Christmas cards witness to the beauty of a white Christmas, there is nothing sentimental about the scene depicted here. The repeated 'snow on snow' is simply bitter; it is about weather that is pitiless and dangerous to life.

The second verse turns to a reflection on 'Our God', evoking the Incarnation in the beautiful phrase 'Heaven cannot hold Him'. This echoes Solomon's prayer in 1 Kings 8.27, where the king, who is dedicating the Temple, acknowledges: 'Behold, heaven, and the highest heaven, cannot contain you.' This is about conceding that God's greatness will never be simply located in any one place, such as the Temple. But the simplicity of the word 'hold' in the poem works slightly differently. It is as if the normal boundaries of reality have been crucially broken by the action of God. The heavens (the place of God's reign) could not hang onto the wild, risk-taking generosity of God who has literally fallen to earth to be with his beloved people. The second two lines move smoothly from the incarnation to the expectation of the second coming: 'Heaven and earth shall flee away/ When he comes to reign.' With this simple repetition and contrast, the poet picks up and celebrates the themes of Advent and Christmas together (the power and judgement, the total vulnerability), all done in 20 succinct words.

The middle verse picks up the thought that was begun a few lines before, namely that 'a stable-place sufficed' the Lord of earth and heaven. This stanza starts directly with the astonishing word 'Enough'. Coming into a context of dire human need, this our God finds what is offered to the baby 'enough' in terms of provision, love and worship. The contrast between the courts of heaven and the conditions in the stable are stressed in both halves of the verse.

The ceaseless praise of cherubim and angels is matched with what a woman's body can give for sustenance; what hay, the most meagre and uncomfortable of beddings, can provide for warmth; and what a bevy of smelly working animals can offer in terms of attention. The graphic animal physicality of it is important: no other carol that gets sung in church actually mentions Mary's breasts, and what they are for. The next verse reinforces this human devotion, this response to the baby God in his utter need. The hosts of heaven are obliged to leave their proper realm and throng the air on earth, to witness this miracle. Again, Mary's role as privileged provider, just like any other mother with a newborn, is stressed. She gets to kiss the baby, and this is profound worship. Notice that the child is named 'the Beloved'; this is a love poem to God.

Finally there is the question of the narrator's response (and, it is implied, our own). Here the shepherds and wise men make their first entrance in the poem, as if we enter the stable along with them and need to consider what we are bringing with us as we come. The poverty of the narrator is, I think, intended to reflect a different kind of poverty from the austerity depicted in the poem; it is a poverty of response to the grace of God. The whole poem has been an exercise in taking the reader to the manger, and by so doing deepening our reaction to the astonishing wonder of what has taken place. It is intended to touch our hearts, not just with awe, but with love.

If you have a favourite carol, read the words of it slowly, as with a poem.

27 December

Christmas

All after pleasures as I rid one day,
     My horse and I, both tired, body and mind,
     With full cry of affections, quite astray;
I took up in the next Inn I could find.

There when I came, whom found I but my dear,
     My dearest Lord, expecting till the grief
     Of pleasures brought me to him, ready there
To be all passengers' most sweet relief?

O Thou, whose glorious, yet contracted light,
     Wrapt in night's mantle, stole into a manger;
     Since my dark soul and brutish is thy right,
To Man of all beasts be not thou a stranger:

Furnish and deck my soul, that thou may'st have
A better lodging, than a rack, or grave.

The shepherds sing; and shall I silent be?
       My God, no hymn for thee?
My soul's a shepherd too: a flock it feeds
       Of thoughts, and words, and deeds.
The pasture is thy word; the streams, thy grace
       Enriching all the place.

Shepherd and flock shall sing, and all my powers
       Out-sing the daylight hours.
Then we will chide the Sun for letting night
       Take up his place and right:

We sing one common Lord; wherefore he should
>>>>Himself the candle hold.

I will go searching, till I find a Sun
>>>>Shall stay, till we have done;
A willing shiner, that shall shine as gladly,
>>>>As frost-nipt Suns look sadly.
Then we will sing, and shine all our own day,
>>>>And one another pay:

His beams shall cheer my breast, and both so twine,
Till even his beams sing, and my music shine.

>>>>>>*George Herbert*

Herbert's poem is an extended meditation on how to receive the coming of Jesus into one's own soul; this is the meaning of the Incarnation here and now. As is frequently the case with Herbert, there is an interesting experiment here with poetic form. The poem falls into two halves. The first part is a 14-line sonnet; the second half is like an extended sonnet (with an extra six-line stanza in it). Each part resolves into a rhyming couplet, first in the centre of the poem and then at the end. So the reader gets a sense of the second half replying to the first, but with variation and a different mood. The initial sonnet goes inward towards the darkness, and the images developed are all around the stable scene; the second half seems to go outward, via the image of the shepherds, to the landscape and the growing sunlight. Yet all the images explored represent a dimension of the human soul greeting and receiving Christ, and being transformed thereby.

The poem starts not with any conscious wish to 'go to Bethlehem', but with an image of hunting, an activity that stands for the dubious 'pleasures' of the world. In Herbert's time, hunting with dogs would probably not have attracted accusations of animal cruelty, but those who dedicated a lot of time to it were often seen as self-indulgent and spendthrift. This particular hunt appears to have been a waste of time: horse and rider are exhausted, and the hounds have lost the scent ('quite astray') – it is time to find a local hostelry and recuperate. So it is a good image of any pursuit that promises fun but delivers only dissatisfaction all round. The second line implies that the horse and rider are respectively images of the body and the mind, and the hounds, in 'full cry', are the heart's affections that yearn for satisfaction but are actually all over the place and do not know what they really need. We may ourselves be conscious of having overindulged over the holiday feasting.

The next four lines find the narrator coming across his Lord, already at the inn that he has happened to make his stopping place, just as if the Lord was waiting for ('expecting') him to arrive right there. We have the interesting expression 'the grief/ Of pleasures', which is an arresting and paradoxical idea. Yet it is often true that activities that seem pleasurable initially can end in tiredness and regret. The poet is acute in observing that it is precisely at the point of 'grief' that the human soul can finally become aware of the presence of God.

We then move into what is in effect a beautiful prayer to the incarnate God, 'whose glorious, yet contracted light,/ Wrapt in night's mantle, stole into a manger'. Here we have an image of light wrapped up in darkness, as if arriving for a secret assignation, and just appearing there in the manger when no one was looking. With great economy, Herbert embraces the profound theological truth of 'our God contracted to a span' (Charles Wesley), and resolves the light/darkness opposition in a way that sees both as positive. At the same time (as in his surprising presence when we are ready to turn from lesser things), the initiative and the element of surprise is God's. Then, in the answering part of this stanza, the narrator defines his own soul as 'dark' and 'brutish' (like the stable, the domain of animal affections), and yet, because of the precedent of the holy stable, an appropriate place for God to accept hospitality. The first half of the poem ends with a plea to 'Furnish and deck my soul' – just as homes will have been decked out for Christmas. There is a hint of the crucifixion to come ('a rack, or grave'); but the 'rack' could also be a wall-mounted manger. The poet is perhaps characterizing his own heart as rather a gloomy place.

The second half of the poem suddenly introduces the shepherds who were present in the stable, and they are singing. Having asked to have his soul decked to make a 'better lodging' for his Lord, the focus is on his own lack of exuberant response: 'My God, no hymn for thee?' A number of poems by Herbert seem to explore and dwell on melancholy and depression, and in this condition it appears that making poems was hard for him, so the image of 'singing' is perhaps related to this. The poem now picks up the idea of the shepherds and characterizes the human soul as being like a shepherd, handling a flock 'Of thoughts, and words, and deeds', feeding on the pasture of God's word and enriched with the divine streams of grace. It is impossible to avoid thinking of those biblical passages that evoke a pastoral scene, perhaps particularly Psalm 23, which speaks of 'green pastures' and of the restoring of the soul, even in the context of the 'valley of the shadow of death'.

The narrator proclaims that 'Shepherd and flock shall sing'; it is an image of integration, with all parts of himself united in a hymn of praise. There is a sense that his daily life is to become an endless act of prayer that occupies all the daylight hours. He imagines 'chiding' the sun that has given way to night – inevitable in the short daylight of winter, but symbolizing the reign of darkness (he has earlier called his soul 'dark' and 'brutish'). But the 'common Lord' (that is, the God whom both the poet and the sun itself bear witness to) is the same one who arrived to hallow the darkness, 'wrapt in night's mantle'. Now he humbly holds a candle as night falls.

Finally the poem plays with an extended image of the sun as God's blessing – a 'willing shiner' that contrasts with the 'frost-nipt Suns' that will have been an inevitable part of winter so far, representing those times when God seems far away. There is undoubtedly a serious pun here too, referencing 'the Son' who comes as the light of the world. As we move further from the December solstice, the days lengthen and the sunlight grows stronger. The shining of the light and the 'music' made by the poet seem to intertwine, so that the light sings and the poetry shines, mirroring a loving encounter with God, born anew in the soul.

Are you conscious of having overindulged in pleasures? How can you refocus on the work of Christmas in your heart?

28 December

Innocent's Song

Who's that knocking on the window,
Who's that standing at the door,
What are all those presents
Lying on the kitchen floor?

Who is the smiling stranger
With hair as white as gin,
What is he doing with the children
And who could have let him in?

Why has he rubies on his fingers,
A cold, cold crown on his head,
Why, when he caws his carol,
Does the salty snow run red?

Why does he ferry my fireside
As a spider on a thread,
His fingers made of fuses
And his tongue of gingerbread?

Why does the world before him
Melt in a million suns,
Why do his yellow, yearning eyes
Burn like saffron buns?

Watch where he comes walking
Out of the Christmas flame,
Dancing, double-talking:

Herod is his name.

Charles Causley

The well-loved twentieth-century Cornish poet Charles Causley was self-taught, and pursued a poetic style throughout his life that used older rhythmic, rhyming forms such as the ballad. He was unfashionable in the modernist literary critical mainstream, but popular with those who found his directness appealing and accessible, and his works have often been set to music. His poems look simple or even naive on the surface, but, like those of his inspiration William Blake, they are found to have unusual power and depth on further reflection.

'Innocent's Song' addresses the subject of today's fearful feast day in the Christian calendar, Herod's 'massacre of the innocents' – when he sent his soldiers to kill all the boys under two years old in Bethlehem. The arrival of the wise men in Jerusalem alerted Herod (a Jewish king who was a client of the Roman occupying power) to the prophecies about a new king – perhaps one who would challenge his dynasty – to be born in Bethlehem. He asked to be kept informed, pretending that he also wished to worship the child. The atrocity is a dimension of the birth narrative in Matthew (2.16–23) that is seldom read out in church, and finds no traditional place in nativity scenes; we have angels but no soldiers in sight. However, the Church in medieval times was more robust, or perhaps more willing to include violent local politics in the sphere of what Christ came to redeem. The Coventry Carol ('Lully, lullay') is in the form of the lullaby but is almost exclusively devoted to telling the story of the massacre. In a world where abuse of children has been revealed to be much more extensive than we wanted to believe, and indeed where we frequently witness the slaughter of children, whether caught up in conflict or deliberately targeted by deranged gunmen, we might do well to address what are the roots of violence against children.

The poem has six regular, rhymed stanzas with a rhythm like a drumbeat. Five of them consist of questions, which could be coming out of the mouth of an innocent child, wanting an explanation from an adult about a figure who is strange and offers mixed messages about his intentions. All the questions remain unanswered until the ending, and even then, it is only to name him, not to explain. As we shall see, the questions become more and more apocalyptic as the poem proceeds.

The first stanza starts innocently enough and even calls to mind the tradition that it is Christ himself, in the guise of a poor stranger, who may be knocking on our window asking for hospitality, echoing 'Behold, I stand at the door and knock' (Revelation 3.20). But then our eyes are turned to the 'presents/ Lying on the kitchen floor?' It is hard to know how to read this question. Is it Christmas time, and this is an intruder who has scattered the presents around as he searches the house? Is there any suggestion of the gifts brought by the magi? Has the stranger at the door, who may be benign, brought gifts with him – in which case, why are they lying on the floor? The second stanza, however, confirms that there is something sinister going on. At one level he is 'smiling', but his hair is 'white as gin' (why is that so threatening?). Then comes the only direct reference to a threat to the children, menacingly asked: 'What is he doing with the children/ And who could have let him in?' The technique of expressing horror through unanswered questions alone leaves the reader's imagination to do the bulk of the work.

By the time we arrive at the third stanza, the figure, robed in the paraphernalia of royalty, almost seems like someone in fancy dress, since the references to the 'kitchen floor' and the 'fireside' seem to suggest a contemporary dwelling. Yet this overdressed reveller, who himself seems to sing carols (yet hear that extraordinary alliterative word 'caws' – like an ominous, tuneless raven), suddenly turns lethal.

The rubies on his fingers – a sign of wealth and royalty – already seem to predict the blood that is staining the snow by the end of the verse. The 'cold, cold crown' speaks of the chilling decisions made by those who wield political power and are determined to hold onto it, however cold-hearted the means of doing so.

The fourth stanza continues the confusing, blended messages given off by this creature: does he represent fun or a major threat? Does he bring teatime treats or leave explosions in his wake? And this morphs into a global horror when the spider spinning its web across the fireside suddenly becomes a figure capable of detonating atom bombs with the power of 'a million suns'. Yet still there are confusing mentions of sweet cakes – his yellow eyes are 'like saffron buns'. Innocent temptation and global horror are yoked together.

The final stanza is a warning against the 'double-talking' Herod, who comes in the wake of Christmas celebrations (the 'real world' reasserting itself, after all this sentimental nonsense about 'peace on earth'?). In this verse we have the pause of a line space between the description of this dancing, threatening figure who cannot be separated from the beautiful candlelight of Christmas, and the first explicit mention of his name. But we should not give house room to the 'business as usual' cold-blooded politics that pursues its path over the bodies of children, pretending this is the inevitable price of reality.

Which person or group would you see as a modern-day Herod?

29 December

Song for a Winter Birth

Under the watchful lights
    A child was born;
From a mortal house of flesh
    Painfully torn.

And we, who later assembled
    To praise or peer,
Saw merely an infant boy
    Sleeping there.

Till he awoke and stretched
    Small arms wide
And for food or comfort
    Quavering cried.

A cry and attitude
    Rehearsing in small
The deathless death still haunting
    The Place of the Skull.

Outside, in the festive air,
    We lit cigars.
The night was nailed to the sky
    With hard bright stars.

Vernon Scannell

Vernon Scannell was born in Lincolnshire in 1922 to a poor family and left school at 14, later becoming self-taught in both reading and writing poetry. He used to quote with approval A. E. Housman's comment about poetry: 'The business of poetry is to harmonize the sadness of the universe.' His poem about 'a winter birth' seems to reflect this. It is, like Rossetti's 'Christmas Carol', composed in very simple language with brief, almost terse lines. There are five four-line verses, with the second and fourth lines always rhyming with each other. A sense of inevitability and finality is found as we reach the last line of each stanza, and there is frequently an uncomfortable conclusion. The Christian celebration of Christmas Day is followed immediately by painful feast days: 26 December is St Stephen's Day, commemorating the first martyr among those who made up the early Church, and yesterday (28th) the Church remembered the Holy Innocents, the children massacred by Herod. Today it is the turn of Thomas Becket, who defied his king and was assassinated in Canterbury Cathedral. The tone of this poem is appropriate in this context.

It is not easy to determine who is meant by the 'we' of the poem's narration, or even whether the birth described is a contemporary event or the nativity of the Christchild in the stable. In verse two, 'We, who later assembled' could be the magi, but the 'cigars' of the last verse certainly suggest the modern era; and the reference to the 'Place of the Skull' implies a knowledge of Jesus' life and death that would not have been available to the wise men. Nevertheless, precisely because of this reference, we have to conclude that the Christchild is either the subject of the poem or is consciously called to mind by the presence of the contemporary baby. So it is likely to be intentional that the reader should be thinking about both eras simultaneously.

The first stanza speaks about 'watchful lights'; I suppose these could be the stars mentioned at the end of the poem – but those are 'outside'. So these lights could be the lights of an operating theatre, under which a difficult forceps birth or even a Caesarean was performed, 'painfully torn'. There is even the possibility that we are talking about a birth that has occurred in wartime conditions, since the idea could be of 'watch lights'. The atmosphere is fraught with pain. The mother's womb is called 'a mortal house of flesh'. There is an echo of John Milton's description of the Incarnation in his poem 'Ode on the Morning of Christ's Nativity', where he says that the Son of God 'Forsook the courts of everlasting day,/ And chose with us a darksome house of mortal clay'. Scannell's re-use of the image, linked to painful tearing, takes us out of the realm of ponderous, formal poetry into the graphic reality of what even an ordinary birth is actually like.

The next verse is spoken in the voice of someone who has come to see the baby, but has a certain detachment about the whole thing. The tone does not really suggest the perspective of the magi, who according to tradition travelled many miles over many months to find the one they were seeking; there is no passion here. Nevertheless, there is a sense of surprise at seeing 'merely an infant boy'; the magi had originally looked for the child in a king's palace. The poet's alliterative linking of 'to praise or to peer' manages to suggest a whole range of reasons why one would go and see a baby. It allows for the sense of devotion, but also for the half-hearted inspection by an unenthusiastic (male) relation of a newborn baby in the family – an excuse to get out the cigars, but not much more exciting than that. But note the line 'Sleeping there'; it is a touch of gentleness in an otherwise hard poem, where it is implied that the onlookers are themselves rather hard-hearted, or at least uncomfortable and well out of their depth.

The central stanza has the baby suddenly waking, and crying with that very particular 'quavering', fragile sound of the newborn. Evidence that the poet has personally observed the very newly born is there in the description of the sudden flinging apart of his arms that the child instinctively enacts – this is one of the reflexes that is tested to check that a baby is developing normally. It looks rather dramatic and the child often 'freezes' in the pose that, in the next stanza, the narrator compares with the stance of the crucified body. He expresses how the child's attitude rehearses the 'deathless death still haunting/ The Place of the Skull'. (The 'place of the skull' is the meaning of the name Golgotha, the traditional site of the crucifixion.) There is something very poignant about pointing out how the pose shows this forth 'in small' – this is a very tiny baby, barely arrived and already practising for his death. This poem does something that was totally traditional in medieval carols, namely to weave together the stories of Jesus' birth and his violent death; Christian devotion did not, until later, more sentimental times, let us indulge purely in baby-worship.

The final verse seems to locate us in the contemporary world, in a modern gathering in response to a birth (a christening perhaps?). It is as if the narrator and those with him repair outside to smoke celebration cigars, and while there they gaze at the sky. We are left with an image that is highly visual, depicting a sky that, in the clear and frosty air, is full of stars. But the arresting, violent metaphor at the end is that 'the night was nailed to the sky' with the stars, as Christ was nailed to the cross. The poet allows us no relief here.

Are there any personal reasons for you that make Christmas a hard time of the year?

30 December

Musée des Beaux Arts

About suffering they were never wrong,
The Old Masters: how well they understood
Its human position; how it takes place
While someone else is eating or opening a window or just walking
    dully along;
How, when the aged are reverently, passionately waiting
For the miraculous birth, there always must be
Children who did not specially want it to happen, skating
On a pond at the edge of the wood:
They never forgot
That even the dreadful martyrdom must run its course
Anyhow in a corner, some untidy spot   .
Where the dogs go on with their doggy life and the torturer's horse
Scratches its innocent behind on a tree.

In Breughel's *Icarus*, for instance: how everything turns away
Quite leisurely from the disaster; the ploughman may
Have heard the splash, the forsaken cry,
But for him it was not an important failure; the sun shone
As it had to on the white legs disappearing into the green
Water; and the expensive delicate ship that must have seen
Something amazing, a boy falling out of the sky,
Had somewhere to get to and sailed calmly on.

December 1938

W. H. Auden

This poem seems to me to chime with the slightly reflective, 'limbo' feeling of the days between Christmas and New Year. It is set as if the narrator is in the Royal Museum of Fine Arts in Belgium, and proceeds as a sort of reflection on the musings of someone looking at the pictures on display, using what he has in front of him to generalize about the wisdom of painters usually regarded as 'old masters'. The tone is conversational and detached, and this echoes the theme of the poem, which is that dramatic events of great mythological or religious significance, when envisaged in the midst of an ordinary landscape, must have occurred without most people who were around at the time even noticing them or considering them important.

Only one work is actually named, depicting the fall of Icarus, who famously tried to fly with wings made by his father, the master-artificer Daedalus. These were stuck together with wax, but Icarus flew too close to the sun, the wax melted, the wings failed and he was plunged into the sea. The painting was thought to be by Pieter Breughel the Elder, but is now believed to be a copy. But there are clearly other paintings referred to in the poem too: there is one of a religious martyrdom of some sort (perhaps a St Sebastian?), and then the jewel in the museum's crown, the *Census at Bethlehem* by Breughel. All these images, particularly the latter, are full of complex incidental activities surrounding the main, holy event. The figure of Mary on the donkey, approaching the stable, is actually quite hard to pick out, and indeed children are skating on the pond nearby, quite oblivious. But many other pictures may be in there, depicting people eating, or opening a window, and so on. The narrator seems to be moving from picture to picture – either within the museum or by calling a number of 'old masters' to mind – with a neutrality of response that does not vary as different images are inspected. Sometimes this neutrality is shocking – what does it mean, for instance, to refer to a torturer's horse as 'innocent'? Of course the animal is not responsible for the atrocity, but the bland tone apparently invites us not to react. There is heavy irony here; if we miss it we become part of the world that ignores the significance of the event.

The poem begins by seeming to announce that it is 'about suffering'; and readers of this poem who have experienced tragedy of various kinds will be able to testify that there is a curious sort of comfort in the observations of this laconic narrator. Suffering does indeed take place while the rest of the world is quietly, or noisily, going about its business, just as if the world-changing personal events were not happening or did not matter – this is recognizably the 'human position' of those who suffer. But then, before going into the details of the pictures showing tragedies, the narrator seems to spend a moment gazing at the scene where the nativity is just about to happen. It is as if the 'miraculous birth' is classically set in a context where what we are reflecting about is suffering. As we have seen from some of the poetry that tackles the nativity head-on, this is indeed the context of the Incarnation; it is not a protected space divorced from local realities of politics and time. It has been suggested that in the depiction of the census at Bethlehem, Breughel is making some points about the severity of the Spanish administration in the southern Netherlands at the time (1566).

The narrator allows for huge differences in the human response to the event of the Incarnation: the aged are 'reverently, passionately waiting' (we may think of Simeon and Anna in Luke 2.25–38), but there are also 'Children who did not specially want it to happen'. These children are like the people and animals featured (some prominently) in the other pictures, who turn away from the main event, not with hostility but complete indifference. They simply have other agendas: an icy pond to enjoy, a 'doggy life' to pursue, a backside to scratch, a field to plough, somewhere else to get to. Humans and animals are lumped together, suggesting that the majority of people have no more capacity for empathy or insight about what is really happening than does a child or a puppy. There is even a kind of implied innocence in this immersion in the life of the physical, this lowering of horizons.

The poem's structure is interesting. Its conversational tone is reflected in its irregular line length, which takes on the meaning of what is being said (note how the line that ends 'walking dully along' seems to meander on for ever). But there is something careful happening with the rhyme scheme. Most of the line endings find a rhyming echo coming back at some point (just as the generalization made by the narrator finds anecdotal back-up from more than one picture). But in the last eight lines the rhyme structure becomes more strict and focused (AABCDDBC), giving the sense that something important is being resolved (this is the nature of suffering), even as we hear that an astonishing event – a boy falling out of the sky – was simply not attended to by anyone who could have witnessed it at the time. The viewer of that picture is indeed placed in the same position as the witnesses, since the death of the boy is in the remote distance, while the work of the ploughman takes up the whole foreground. The boy gives a 'forsaken cry' before sinking beneath the waves, reminiscent of Christ's cry on the cross.

What are we asked to make of this poem, with its well-observed incidental details of visual images and its deadpan tone? At one level it is simply mirroring the technique of the paintings it is referring to, where the 'dreadful martyrdom' and the 'doggy life' can be represented with equal focus. But at another, it may implicitly be commenting on the political realities of the world in which it was written. It was published in 1938, during the build-up to the Second World War. Auden was acutely conscious of the dangers of fascism, and also the way in which people were trying to avoid noticing what was happening, even though it was potentially cataclysmic. Reading the poem in our own day, we should consider whether we too simply turn away 'Quite leisurely' from events of huge significance, because we have 'somewhere to get to'.

As you reflect on the past year, do you think that there is anything potentially cataclysmic occurring in the world, which people are trying not to notice?

31 December

————•◦•————

'Ring out, wild bells'

Ring out, wild bells, to the wild sky,
    The flying cloud, the frosty light:
    The year is dying in the night;
Ring out, wild bells, and let him die.

Ring out the old, ring in the new,
    Ring, happy bells, across the snow:
    The year is going, let him go;
Ring out the false, ring in the true.

Ring out the grief that saps the mind,
    For those that here we see no more;
    Ring out the feud of rich and poor,
Ring in redress to all mankind.

Ring out a slowly dying cause,
    And ancient forms of party strife;
    Ring in the nobler modes of life,
With sweeter manners, purer laws.

Ring out the want, the care, the sin,
    The faithless coldness of the times;
    Ring out, ring out my mournful rhymes,
But ring the fuller minstrel in.

Ring out false pride in place and blood,
    The civic slander and the spite;
    Ring in the love of truth and right,
Ring in the common love of good.

Ring out old shapes of foul disease;
    Ring out the narrowing lust of gold;
    Ring out the thousand wars of old,
Ring in the thousand years of peace.

Ring in the valiant man and free,
    The larger heart, the kindlier hand;
    Ring out the darkness of the land,
Ring in the Christ that is to be.

Alfred, Lord Tennyson

Alfred, Lord Tennyson was an immensely popular poet in his times. He seems to have been able to articulate an emotional vocabulary that was hugely appealing to the Victorians – indeed Queen Victoria herself is said to have derived much consolation after Prince Albert's death from the long poem from which these stanzas are taken. They form just a small part of 'In Memoriam AHH', which was composed over a number of years in honour of Tennyson's much loved friend Arthur Hallam, who died at the age of 23. It was published in 1850, the year Tennyson was made poet laureate. Throughout, each stanza has a regular three-beat line (a tetrameter), and an ABBA rhyme scheme. It is so characteristic that this form is now called an 'In Memoriam stanza'. For modern tastes it is extremely long and unvaried, but the poem as a whole ranges over many subjects including the philosophical and scientific; for instance it shows knowledge of the current debates about evolution ('Nature red in tooth and claw'). But the dominant theme is about coming to terms with untimely death and grief. Arthur Hallam was to have married Tennyson's sister, and so the sense of someone missing is experienced within the whole family. Within the sequence of cantos, Christmas celebrations, marred because of Arthur's absence, are several times referred to; and the season is usually marked by the sound of church bells, traditionally rung for the festivals.

This sequence describes the bells as 'wild', ringing out to the 'wild sky'. Some have suggested that this was not a deliberate peal of bells, but the result of a storm that disturbed a set of bells and created a cacophony. However, it seems more likely, in context, that this is a meditation set at Christmas time or on the cusp of the year, and that the poem, with its insistent, regular repetitions, is seeking to reflect a formal, long drawn-out peal. The 'wildness' echoes the passion of the unresolvable major grief that the whole poem bears witness to. The words 'let him die', in relation to the old year that is passing, derive some of their force from the grief about a friend's death and the bleak pain of having to let him go. The poet draws on these emotions to speak of a wider canvas of human yearnings and wrongdoing, and so the poem is one that has often spoken to readers at the turn of the year.

The second stanza has a certain jollity about it, the epitome of a Victorian Christmas scene: 'Ring, happy bells, across the snow'; and there is a straightforward sense that we can hope to 'Ring out the false, ring in the true'. It sounds rather simplistic. But later stanzas, while remaining quite generalized, call forth a list of unwanted negative realities that are wholly believable and very hard to shake off: personal 'grief that saps the mind'; class conflict ('the feud of rich and poor', 'false pride in place and blood'); tedious and inflexible political stand-offs ('a slowly dying cause', 'ancient forms of party strife'); a hostile and alienated culture and press ('the faithless coldness of the times', 'the civic slander and the spite'); epidemics and diseases that medicine cannot seem to conquer; an unhealthy attachment to personal wealth as the only value worth striving for ('the narrowing lust of gold'); and endless, endless wars. Well might the poet dream of ringing out these things with the passing of the old year; it appears today that they have never gone out of fashion.

The narrator even wants to 'ring out my mournful rhymes', and the need for them. Each stanza ends with the positive good that is wanted: truth, redress for all, 'sweeter manners', a 'common love of good', 'The larger heart, the kindlier hand'. As ever, it is much easier and more convincing to name what feels wrong than to explain in detail the good that is desired. But the repeated cry 'Ring out . . . Ring in . . .' has an energy and a charge that allows us to inhabit a real hope that things can indeed change, and a conviction that part of what is needed for this to happen is a fundamental shift in the aspirations of the human heart. It is not surprising that some of these verses were used by the composer Karl Jenkins in his oratorio *The Armed Man*, as a rousing clarion call to peace after the turmoil and suffering of war.

But it is in the last two stanzas that the apocalyptic nature of the vision is made clear. These may be Christmas bells, but the hope is for a 'thousand years of peace', and for 'the Christ that is to be', not simply as a child in the manger but as the ruling sovereign of the end times. Once again, the promise of Advent and Christmas is not merely the memory of a poignant winter birth, but the hope of the world's salvation throughout all time.

What are your hopes for yourself and for the world in the coming year?

1 January

---•◦•---

The Year's Midnight

The flown, the fallen,
the golden ones,
the deciduous dead, all gone
to ground, to dust, to sand,
borne on the shoulders of the wind.

Listen! They are whispering
now while the world talks,
and the ice melts,
and the seas rise.
Look at the trees!

Every leaf-scar is a bud
expecting a future.
The earth speaks in parables.
The burning bush. The rainbow.
Promises. Promises.

Gillian Clarke

At the turn of the year, it is especially poignant to remember those
we love who have died. If they have died during the year that is just
ending, there is the sense that we are leaving them behind in that
year, while we are forced to move on; there is an increased sense
of distance from the beloved dead, as the year that saw the event of
their death officially becomes history. With a major bereavement,
and perhaps especially that of a child or adolescent who is now per-
petually and unchangingly young (unlike ourselves), each new year

increases the age difference between us and them. And as we grow older, we have more names to remember as the company of family and friends who have died naturally increases, and we become more conscious of the passing of those of our own generation and above who were household names. It is a moment when we tend to take stock of how many new years we ourselves are likely to see.

This brief poem by Gillian Clarke starts with the memory of these, 'The flown, the fallen,/ the golden ones' – an interesting list of ways to characterize the dead. 'Flown' and 'fallen' are such contrasting metaphors: the first suggests freedom, migration, upward flight and almost a sudden decision to go; the second suggests being cut down in the midst of life and duties (like a serving soldier), unable to survive a fatal danger. 'The golden ones' probably embraces those who in life shone on a wider canvas but who succumbed, as we all do, to mortality. The phrase has echoes of Shakespeare's 'golden lads and girls' who 'all must/ Like chimneysweepers come to dust' (*Cymbeline* IV.ii.258). Then, after fairly conventional adjectives, comes the brilliant word 'deciduous', which alliterates with 'dead'. It encompasses that sense of natural inevitability about dying, as well as the sadness of the bare trees after leaf fall. It is normal for deciduous trees to shed leaves in the winter, after a short summer season. It is normal for humans to die, after a poignantly short span of glorious life. Notice the slight pause that the line break gives to the assertion of finality: 'all gone/ to ground, to dust, to sand'. The threefold repetition echoes the threefold characterization of the dead as 'flown', 'fallen', 'golden'. When compared with other poems that contemplate inevitable mortality (for instance Shelley's 'Ozymandias', p. 41), it's worth noticing the distinctive mood here. Instead of irony or despair, there is a sense of rightness, even of gentleness about the process of dying and decay. The dead are 'borne on the shoulders of the wind' like sand, even though they are truly 'gone'.

The second stanza changes tack entirely, cutting through the reverie of the first. Having been made one with the earth, the dead seem to return to us like the voice of the planet itself. The narrator imagines them 'whispering/ now while the world talks'. The image is of the guiding voices of the dead trying to communicate urgency about climate change to us who are alive and able to act, but whether the implication is that human culture is talking about other things (and so is oblivious to these whispered warnings), or that the planet itself is beginning to 'talk' to us in the same vein, I am not sure. New year is a time when we contemplate a change in our habits and take stock of the direction we are going in personally or as a society. These days it is also a key time when we may be experiencing the extremes of weather that seem to herald threatening developments in the biosphere (the melting of the Arctic sea ice) that may or may not be reversible in the future, depending on how we live and plan for that. But the stanza ends with an appeal to 'Look at the trees!'

The life-cycle of deciduous trees has provided powerful metaphors, in this selection of poems, of dieback and withdrawal in the face of darkness. But the third stanza highlights the promise of new life: 'Every leaf-scar is a bud/ expecting a future.' It is the case that the buds are already nascent as the leaves of autumn are pulled away by the wind, but at the start of January (especially if the season has been mild), it becomes more obvious that they are ready to break again, even if they will not do so yet. And so the narrator of this poem, having given a warning, yet returns to the sense of hope we find in the natural cycle, even if for us, like these trees, it includes death and decay. It is as if there is real communication between us and the earth, although it may be puzzling and not straightforward. The poet invokes biblical echoes: 'The earth speaks in parables.' Parables, famously the teaching method used by Jesus, offer a story we have to interpret ourselves and not a moral that can be easily read off and obeyed. The insight has to be worked for, the understanding fully engaged; and there is no certainty that our interpretation is final or right.

The poem recalls two biblical narratives (actually not themselves parables, but stories that have long seized the imaginations of religious followers). Both feature phenomena that are observed in the landscape. Moses the shepherd encounters a bush in the desert that appears to burn without being consumed. He turns aside and a voice from heaven declares that he is on 'holy ground'. Here the name and nature of God are revealed to him and he is given the commission to lead his people out of slavery (Exodus 3.1–12). And the rainbow is the culmination of the story of Noah and his family and animals, who are the only ones saved from the great flood. The rainbow is said to be the evidence in the sky of God's promise to his people that the earth and its creatures will never again be destroyed by a natural disaster (Genesis 9.10–17). So the stories contain some of the greatest promises of religious faith. But the poet leaves us without any certainty. The repetition 'Promises. Promises' uses the colloquial phrase that casts doubt on the reliability of assurances at the same time as announcing their existence.

In a poem that could not be more different from Tennyson's extremely lengthy meditation on personal grief, human society, scientific knowledge and religious faith, Clarke has succeeded, with great economy, in touching on all of these.

Who is the most important of your beloved dead? From your memories of them, what gives you hope for the future?

2 January

----·•·----

Agnus Dei

Given that lambs
are infant sheep, that sheep
are afraid and foolish, and lack
the means of self-protection, having
neither rage nor claws,
venom nor cunning,
what then
is this 'Lamb of God'?

This pretty creature, vigorous
to nuzzle at milky dugs,
woolbearer, bleater,
leaper in air for delight of being, who finds in astonishment
four legs to land on, the grass
all it knows of the world?
                    With whom we would like to play,
whom we'd lead with ribbons, but may not bring
into our houses because
it would soil the floor with its droppings?

What terror lies concealed
in strangest words, *O lamb*
of God that taketh away
the Sins of the World: an innocence
          smelling of ignorance
          born in bloody snowdrifts,
          licked by forebearing
dogs more intelligent than its entire flock put together?

2 January

God then,
encompassing all things, is
defenseless? Omnipotence
has been tossed away, reduced
to a wisp of damp wool?

                    And we
frightened, bored, wanting
only to sleep till catastrophe
has raged, clashed, seethed and gone by without us,
                    wanting then
to awaken in quietude without remembrance of agony,

                    we who in shamefaced private hope
had looked to be plucked from fire and given
a bliss we deserved for having imagined it,

                    is it implied that *we*
must protect this perversely weak
animal, whose muzzle's nudgings
suppose there is milk to be found in us?
Must hold to our icy hearts
a shivering God?

                    *

So be it.
    Come, rag of pungent
quiverings,
            dim star.
                    Let's try
if something human still
can shield you,
                    spark
of remote light.

Denise Levertov

The first week of January brings us to the earliest period (in a British climate) when lambing is expected among sheep farmers. It is a time of year when both ewes and their lambs can be vulnerable, particularly if conditions are snowy, and so it is not uncommon for the pregnant ewes to be brought indoors before their delivery. This poem shows close observation of very young lambs and their dependence on human care and intervention to protect them at this stage. What Denise Levertov has done is to take a very familiar religious phrase, 'Lamb of God', and explore in detail the realities behind the image.

'Lamb of God' as a phrase has cropped up previously in this volume; Waldo Williams, in his poem about the shepherds (p. 87), describes the event of Christmas as the 'birthday of the Lamb of God'. The application of this name to Jesus has a very ancient heritage. In the Gospel of John, it is the greeting John the Baptist gives to Jesus when he comes for baptism: 'Here is the Lamb of God, who takes away the sin of the world' (John 1.29). As the Latin title of this poem suggests, this expression has found its way into the heart of the Eucharist in Christian liturgy. In the ancient world people would have been familiar with the practices of animal sacrifice in the Temple and would instantly have made the connection with the lamb that every family was instructed to sacrifice and then roast to eat with the Passover meal. It was the sacrifice that in Egypt protected the Jewish people from the plague of the slaying of the firstborn, and it was the harbinger of their deliverance from slavery in Egypt. The Passion narratives in the Gospels all link the death of Jesus with the celebration of Passover; in John's Gospel, events occur exactly on the day that the Passover lambs would have been slaughtered. The Lamb of God appears again in the apocalyptic book of Revelation, as an image of the risen and victorious Saviour.

But Levertov wants to make us look again at the animal that underlies this symbolism, and what its characteristics tell us about the nature of the God who became incarnate. William Blake (whose 'Tyger' poem appears on p. 48), also reflected on the Lamb who gives its name to the Saviour, but this longer meditation forms an interesting contrast. She states the question: since the lamb is not only defenceless and unaggressive but frankly stupid, 'what then/ is this

"Lamb of God"?' She then, in a series of irregular, wide-ranging discursive stanzas, lays bare some of the attitudes (practical and romanticized) we have towards spring lambs, and opens up the paradox of applying any of these observations to almighty God.

The first stanza concentrates on the lamb's sheer cuteness: its distinctive gambolling and leaping movements, its (temporary) attractiveness as a plaything, a creature to dress up and decorate and treat like a pet. This impulse is undercut by remembering about its tendency to leave droppings. It is as if a childish reaction is pulled back by adult practicality. But then the mood makes another sudden lurch, this time into terror and strangeness. The liturgical prayer is put in the context of the smells of animal birth, 'bloody snowdrifts', the protective attentions of animals of superior intelligence. Here is innocence not as chocolate-box cuteness but real helplessness in the face of danger.

There is a brief stanza, with short lines, stating the poem's question afresh. Has the omnipotence of God been 'tossed away, reduced/ to a wisp of damp wool?' It is another way of expressing the incomprehensible self-emptying implied by the incarnation. We have seen the vulnerable, crying child in several poems (Christina Rossetti, p. 94, and Vernon Scannell, p. 106, for example). The newborn lamb, still wet from the womb, as an image of God is even more defenceless and pitiful.

The narrator turns her attention now on us; she is scathing in her critique of the kind of prayers and yearnings that characterize us. We ask to be spared all danger, all catastrophe, to wake up when the agony is over, to be 'plucked from fire' that we never really faced. We prefer to see ourselves as the helpless ones, deserving to avoid sacrifice or hardship – but why? The narrator may be referring to the predictions of conflict and hardship that are said to be the prelude to the end times, or she may be implying that at a personal level we do not expect to face testing and judgement as we go through life. The longing for sleep may recall the inability of Jesus' disciples to stay awake in the Garden of Gethsemane before his Passion (Luke 22.45–46). But some of the references are about Christian lives that have actively taken a harder path than this. John Wesley, who was rescued from a house fire as a child, described himself as a 'brand plucked from the burning', and went on to found the Methodist Church, believing himself specially chosen by God.

So the next question is about ourselves, faced with a God who has the characteristics of a newborn lamb. The helpless creature looks to us for sustenance, asks of us protection and nourishment, expects us to open our icy hearts, offers us a God who is not always almighty but is sometimes shivering with cold. There is a nice onomatopoeia about the insistent 'muzzle's nudgings', reflecting the instinctive determination of the newborn to get what it requires in order to live, and the similar determination of God that we shall respond with compassion to his promptings.

Instead of a glorious Bethlehem star, we have a 'dim star'. Instead of a triumphant dayspring from on high, we have a 'spark/ of remote light'. We are not here called to fall to our knees in adoration, but to take charge and be strong. For the capacity to shield this light is the true test of our humanity in response to the God who is here revealed.

What new responsibility could God be calling you to this year?

3 January

Woman to Child

You who were darkness warmed my flesh
where out of darkness rose the seed.
Then all a world I made in me:
all the world you hear and see
hung upon my dreaming blood.

There moved the multitudinous stars,
and coloured birds and fishes moved.
There swam the sliding continents.
All time lay rolled in me, and sense,
and love that knew not its beloved.

O node and focus of the world –
I hold you deep within that well
you shall escape and not escape –
that mirrors still your sleeping shape,
that nurtures still your crescent cell.

I wither and you break from me;
yet though you dance in living light,
I am the earth, I am the root,
I am the stem that fed the fruit,
the link that joins you to the night.

Judith Wright

Within the birth narratives in Luke's Gospel (chapters 1—2), it is said several times, in relation to the remarkable events, that Mary 'kept all these things, pondering them in her heart' (Luke 2.19). This is true of the arrival and greeting of the angel, the account of the shepherds about the angelic message, the reaction to the infant Jesus when he is presented in the Temple, and the time when Jesus, after his bar-mitzvah in Jerusalem, was found to have stayed behind debating with the rabbis. It is so unusual in biblical narrative to give any sort of window on the interior thoughts of an individual that it has led some to believe that Mary herself must have been Luke's source for the account he gives. Whatever the truth of this, it is an ancient tradition that Mary was reflective about herself and what had happened to her, and about her child and who he was to be.

This poem by the Australian Judith Wright does not specifically address the extraordinary experience of Mary; it could describe that of any woman who has given birth. But it provides a helpful meditation on how the miracle of incarnation through the process of a human birth mirrors the miracle of every generation of new life through pregnancy and birth. The poem is written as if from the perspective of a woman whose child has been born ('you dance in living light'), looking back over her pregnancy and the developing relationship between her and the growing child. The form of the poem is regular but unusual. Each of the four stanzas has five lines, the first of which is unrhymed with any other, but the next four are a reliable ABBA pattern. Each stanza comes to a resolution in the last line, which makes the feel of the poem serene and composed. It also means that the unrhymed first line of the next verse has a special prominence, in each case starting an important new thought.

The first three verses speak of pregnancy, and of that particular, intimate kind of 'unknowing' that it brings: processes essential to life that occur in darkness without the voluntary activity of the mother; and the consequent experience of love and connection with a person who is unseen and unknown. The narrator addresses the child: 'You who were darkness' matches the darkness of the act of conception in the woman's womb. This is a darkness full of creativity, mirroring the action of the divine: 'Then all a world I made in me'. It is difficult to articulate how powerfully the experience of carrying life makes you feel like a living, breathing image of God. It is, of course, the case that for the foetus the womb provides an environment that offers all that it needs, while providing muffled access to the sounds of the world around. The phrase 'dreaming blood' is brilliantly chosen. It is the maternal blood supply that increases in pregnancy and carries nutrients to the child. To give blood the power of dreaming suggests the proactive way in which the involuntary processes do the work of constructing human life and consciousness. In Australian aboriginal thought, 'dreamtime' is a powerful state essential to people's understanding of human identity and its connection with creation.

The second stanza elaborates imaginatively on the internal world created in the body of the mother. I think it captures the mother's feeling of being like God in the creation of a total environment for life, but it also implies that she is the locus for the dreams of the growing child, who will encounter the external creation after birth, and needs to 'dream' them now. But if this verse is applied to Mary, it has a special resonance in that the child who is developing is believed to have been himself the creator of the 'multitudinous stars' and we are contemplating a true paradox of how the body of a woman can contain 'All time . . . and sense . . . and love'. The description of 'love that knew not its beloved' is completely accurate in relation to any pregnant woman and her child, but it also has echoes of the *via negativa* of the soul who seeks to know and love a God who is unknowable except through love.

'O node and focus of the world' is, again, an entirely appropriate impulse of a woman towards the child in her – even if, in literal terms, overstated. But in the heart of Mary, this is not an overstatement but the voice of praise. 'That well/ you shall escape and not escape' speaks of the womb. The experience of motherhood is consciously one in which the woman moves from being all-powerful and all-essential to gradually effacing her own importance more and more, while at the same time exercising appropriate protection. It is a continuous letting go. And yet, though all must escape the womb in order to enter life, there is an eternal pull and yearning to return to a place of total safety and effortless nourishment. The repetition of the word 'still' (half-rhyming with 'well' and 'cell') highlights both continuity and protectiveness – stillness in every sense.

In the last stanza there is an interruption to the smooth 'holding' atmosphere of the previous verses, and this echoes the major disruption of the birth process. It is articulated as a strong independent movement by the child ('you break from me') but also as a sudden obsolescence of the mother, imaged as a plant that dies back after it has successfully fruited ('I wither'). Yet the poem ends on a powerful assertion of the continuing significance of the mother. The narrator affirms herself as the earth, the root, 'the stem that fed the fruit'. In the final line, we return to the 'night', from which this life has sprung and which seems to represent the fertile darkness that gives rise to all life and all creativity.

What of importance have you given birth to in your life, or what do you hope to do?

4 January

―――――•◦•――――

Winter Paradise

Now I am old and free from time
How spacious life,
Unbeginning unending sky where the wind blows
The ever-moving clouds and clouds of starlings on the wing,
Chaffinch and apple-leaf across my garden lawn,
Winter paradise
With its own birds and daisies
And all the near and far that eye can see,
Each blade of grass signed with the mystery
Across whose face unchanging everchanging pass
Summer and winter, day and night.
Great countenance of the unknown known
You have looked upon me all my days,
More loved than lover's face,
More merciful than the heart, more wise
Than spoken word, unspoken theme
Simple as earth in whom we live and move.

Kathleen Raine

In Luke's telling of the story of the birth of Jesus, a special place is given to people of a certain age. Before the story of the annunciation to Mary, there is a similar annunciation to Zechariah, husband of Mary's cousin Elizabeth (Luke 1). Elizabeth conceives John the Baptist at an age when she is past childbearing – a miraculous event that recalls the conception of Isaac to his elderly parents Abraham and Sarah (Genesis 18). After the description of Jesus' nativity, Luke

131

returns us to the Jerusalem Temple for the story of the rite of purifi-
cation following Mary's delivery of her baby (Luke 2.21–38). In the
Temple are two very old people: Anna, a widow of 84, and Simeon,
who has been promised he will not die before he has seen the Lord's
Christ. They recognize the Christchild, and in the story they stand
for those who have devoted their whole lives to watching and
waiting for the presence of God. The Church normally celebrates
this encounter at Candlemas, at the beginning of February.

In our culture it is not at all abnormal for people to live to Anna's
age and well beyond that, and perhaps this is one reason why we are
less inclined to give respect to the wisdom of the elderly and more
likely to regard them as a burdensome demographic time bomb. This
leads many who are entering their later years to try to do everything
they can to continue energetically with the same work and activity that
has always given their lives meaning, until ill health actually prevents
them. However, some ageing people do take the opportunity to shift
and to become more contemplative. They may find that their aware-
ness of the natural world, and perhaps particularly of the changing
seasons, becomes more acute. They take time to notice the landscape,
whose shifting moods become more precious as a person begins to
wonder how many more cycles of the seasons they will experience.

This poem by Kathleen Raine starts with a frank but highly
positive assertion about inhabiting old age. Instead of being seen
as a constriction, it is a time that is 'free from time' – the insistent
demands of deadlines and timetables. The second line, 'How spa-
cious life' is left without any other comment, so that the spacey-ness
of the line reinforces the meaning. From this contemplative space,
the narrator watches the movement of clouds across the face of a
windy sky, along with the birds that gather – the starling commu-
nities – and the individual birds like the chaffinch, and odd leaves
left over from autumn. There is a sense of an endless panorama and
also ceaseless movement and change: a kind of eternity that contains
its own variety. The third and fourth line do not pause for breath, but
the wind blows everything before it; the words ending in 'ing' imply
a state of continuous change that is nevertheless reliably constant,
'unbeginning unending'.

The scene is described as a 'winter paradise'. The puzzling reference to 'daisies' in wintertime could refer to the frost flowers that are created when there has been continuous sub-zero temperatures for several days, building up flower-like patterns in frost upon frost. This would be consistent with the sense that 'each blade of grass is signed with the mystery', since this kind of icy weather picks out individual blades and stalks in an arresting way. But perhaps the phrase describes more than a particular kind of seasonal beauty; the 'winter paradise' could be a state of contentment and contemplation achieved only in the winter of life, in old age.

For the 'mystery' has a face, a 'countenance'. At one level this is simply the earth beneath the grass, over the surface of which pass the seasons in their sequence and the darkness and the light in their daily rhythm. Like the 'unbeginning unending sky', this face is 'unchanging everchanging'. But for the narrator it is something more than the landscape itself. It is the sense of an overarching presence that is benevolent. Personal language is used: this presence has looked upon her 'all my days'; it is 'More loved than lover's face,/ More merciful than the heart, more wise/ Than spoken word'. We have the sense that the narrator has experienced pain as well as passion in love, has suffered grief in her heart, has exchanged a lot of words with others over her lifetime and not felt the wiser for it.

This presence is not defined as God, but it is the 'unknown known', a paradox that has become familiar in this selection of poems. The large number of words in this poem that begin with 'un' keeps offering us ideas that we must negate in order to access their meaning. In this way the poem seeks to point out the limits of words (which, as a writer, her work has depended on), and convey the simplicity of just looking intently at the earth of which she is an accepted part. The final line echoes St Paul's description of God (quoting Epimenides) as the one in whom 'we live and move and have our being' (Acts 17.28).

As you get older, are there any ways in which you feel that your life has become more 'spacious'?

5 January

———————

Journey of the Magi

'A cold coming we had of it,
Just the worst time of the year
For a journey, and such a long journey:
The ways deep and the weather sharp,
The very dead of winter.'
And the camels galled, sore-footed, refractory,
Lying down in the melting snow.
There were times we regretted
The summer palaces on slopes, the terraces,
And the silken girls bringing sherbet.
Then the camel men cursing and grumbling
And running away, and wanting their liquor and women,
And the night-fires going out, and the lack of shelters,
And the cities hostile and the towns unfriendly
And the villages dirty and charging high prices:
A hard time we had of it.
At the end we preferred to travel all night,
Sleeping in snatches,
With the voices singing in our ears, saying
That this was all folly.

Then at dawn we came down to a temperate valley,
Wet, below the snow line, smelling of vegetation,
With a running stream and a water-mill beating the darkness,
And three trees on the low sky.
And an old white horse galloped away in the meadow.
Then we came to a tavern with vine-leaves over the lintel,

Six hands at an open door dicing for pieces of silver,
And feet kicking the empty wine-skins.
But there was no information, and so we continued
And arrived at evening, not a moment too soon
Finding the place; it was (you may say) satisfactory.

All this was a long time ago, I remember,
And I would do it again, but set down
This set down
This: were we led all that way for
Birth or Death? There was a Birth, certainly,
We had evidence and no doubt. I had seen birth and death,
But had thought they were different; this Birth was
Hard and bitter agony for us, like Death, our death.
We returned to our places, these Kingdoms,
But no longer at ease here, in the old dispensation,
With an alien people clutching their gods.
I should be glad of another death.

T. S. Eliot

The journey of the magi, following the star to search out the infant Jesus, is recounted in Matthew's Gospel (Matthew 2), and traditionally celebrated by the Church on the feast of the Epiphany (6 January). Eliot's very famous poem draws on this, but makes a distinctive account from the point of view of one of the magi of a journey made many years ago by an aged speaker who is looking back. He uses the form of a dramatic monologue, where the narrator of the poem is clearly speaking to another person, who does not feature except as an implied listener. It is worth comparing with Matthew Arnold's poem 'Dover Beach' (p. 31), not only for the similar form, but also for a tone of world-weariness, and the sense that previous assumptions have been overturned.

The poem is in three sections. It starts with an almost direct quotation from the 'Sermon on the Nativity' by Lancelot Andrewes of 1622, and it is arresting to notice how in fact that sermon itself speaks in the voice of the magi in a way that makes the listener hear and envisage the concrete conditions of their journey. (Such details are absent from biblical record, and in any case – though some parts of the Middle East can have severe winters – tend to evoke images of muddy, piercingly cold winter journeys in an English landscape.) Andrewes was an English bishop and scholar, and one of the committee that produced the King James translation of the Bible. This accessible way of telling the story to an English congregation enables us to sense some of the creativity that was around at the time, and the importance given to enabling ordinary people to access the biblical text and apply it to their own experience. Eliot's own use of this quotation, and the grumpy monologue that follows, with its wealth of observation and its contemporary mood of alienation, similarly refreshed the telling of the story in the twentieth century.

The first section continues in the same tone as the starting quotation, enumerating the annoyances and difficulties of travel. However, already the details start to have a symbolic significance beyond their concrete reality. At one level we are addressing the discomfort of camels in weather that is much colder than they are used to, making them 'sore-footed, refractory'; at another, we note that the snow is already 'melting', as if the journey is bringing them to a place of renewed warmth and light. The mention of regrets for warmth left behind at home, in their 'summer palaces', seems to emphasize this. There follows a whole list of complaints, no doubt justified but very much in the tone of one who is not used to discomfort and has been accustomed to deferential servants rather than disputatious 'camel men cursing' and dreadful accommodations, if shelter can be found at all. This is clearly someone who, even in old age, will never forget the trials of this particular journey, though the narrator hits on a theme that is recognizable in any generation, including our own, about what it feels like being a foreign tourist and not welcome: 'And the cities hostile and the towns unfriendly/ And the villages dirty and charging high prices.'

The section ends with a description of travelling by night with only snatches of sleep. Instead of speaking of the inspiration and direction provided by the star (indeed the star, a prime mover in the biblical narratives, is not even mentioned in the poem), this magus only recalls 'the voices singing in our ears, saying/ That this was all folly.' This speaker has an almost contemporary kind of cynicism or religious uncertainty about the journey he is engaged in.

The next section, which is still looking back, charts a new phase of the journey as they move into a valley below the snow line, 'smelling of vegetation' (again the hint of fertile new life). This feels like an English or maybe a European landscape, with its watermill on the stream, and the old white horse in the meadow; but the 'three trees on the low sky', while at one level fitting this context, also hint at the three crosses that will be raised on a hill for the crucifixion. The poem leaves out the arrival of the magi in Jerusalem and the conversation with Herod, having them seek for information in this village instead. Although the scene is described naturalistically, further symbols proliferate: the 'vine-leaves' over the lintel of the tavern remind us of the wine of Jesus' last supper, and his claim to his disciples: 'I am the vine, and you are the branches' (John 15.5). The lintel itself hints at the Passover story that underlies the last supper, when the blood of a lamb was daubed on the lintel of the door (Exodus 12.7). The 'dicing for pieces of silver' recalls the soldiers at the foot of the cross who drew lots for Jesus' possessions (John 19.24), and the pieces of silver paid to Judas for betraying his friend (Matthew 26.15). The 'feet kicking the empty wine-skins' recall the parable about needing 'fresh skins' for new wine (Mark 2.22), suggesting that something world-changing has happened, for which we must be ready. However, it is not clear that the speaker is aware of the significance of any of these details.

Finally the narrator recounts their arrival, and even this is described in very downbeat terms: 'it was (you may say) satisfactory'. No mention of the child or his mother, or the traditional gifts opened. The poet is, of course, relying on our deep familiarity with the story, and subverting the reader's expectations by having the speaker provide such a neutral, almost disappointed account. The silence about the child himself has none of the aura of the reticence due to awe; it is more like the dismissiveness of a very old person who is distant from past events, and never felt things very passionately even at the time. It is possible that the poet is commenting on the unengaged nature of much religious observance of his own day.

The final section is spoken as if in the present day to the listener: 'All this was a long time ago'. Here we may be surprised to hear that the speaker believes he would do the journey again. He becomes more reflective, around the connections and correspondences between birth and death. He starts to refer to this Birth with capital letters, and Death as his own death, soon to arrive. But the symbols of crucifixion, and the tradition that has been explored in many other poems, of seeing Jesus' death prefigured in the birth narratives, means that it is another Death (one that was indeed 'hard and bitter agony' that has indeed changed his world). He speaks of a life back home after the journey as one where the magi were 'never at ease', since the birth of the child heralded the death of paganism and magic. And so in spite of himself and a habitual sense of discontent, the speaker reluctantly confesses a kind of faith in the child whose birth he witnessed, a faith that means that he can face his own mortality: 'I should be glad of another death'.

To what extent does entering into the deep themes of Advent, Christmas and Epiphany help you in thinking about your own mortality?

6 January

God's Grandeur

The world is charged with the grandeur of God.
    It will flame out, like shining from shook foil;
    It gathers to a greatness, like the ooze of oil
Crushed. Why do men then now not reck his rod?
Generations have trod, have trod, have trod;
    And all is seared with trade; bleared, smeared with toil;
    And wears man's smudge and shares man's smell; the soil
Is bare now, nor can foot feel, being shod.

And for all this, nature is never spent;
    There lives the dearest freshness deep down things;
And though the last lights off the black West went
    Oh, morning, at the brown brink eastward, springs –
Because the Holy Ghost over the bent
    World broods with warm breast and with ah! bright wings.

Gerard Manley Hopkins

Today is the feast of the Epiphany, when the Church recalls the arrival of the magi to adore the infant Jesus. The term 'epiphany' refers to the 'showing forth' of the glory of God to the Gentiles, since the magi were non-Jews who nevertheless had felt led to search for a newborn king. We still use the word 'epiphany' for an experience of sudden revelation, whether searched for or not – so Hopkins' poem about the manifestation of 'God's grandeur' in the world is especially appropriate on this day.

From his journals we know that Hopkins was highly observant of the natural landscape, and had a strong spiritual response to its

beauty and detail. He was influenced by the work of the philoso-
pher Duns Scotus, who seemed to provide him with a reassurance
that his own poetic sensuousness was a reliable guide to apprehend-
ing the glory of God. Scotus employed the notion of '*haeccitas*' – a
sort of distinctive 'thisness' to individual things, which some have
linked to Hopkins' own theory of 'inscape'. As W. H. Gardner puts it,
'To Hopkins, inscape was something more than a delightful sensory
impression: it was an insight, by divine grace, into the ultimate spir-
itual reality, seeing the pattern, air, melody in things from, as it were,
God's side' (*Scrutiny*, 5(1), July 1936). It is a concept that is coherent
with the Christian belief in the Incarnation.

Whatever his philosophical theory, this poem strongly commu-
nicates a sense of excitement and even exultation in the nature of
things, and their capacity to show forth the glory of God. It is in the
form of a traditional sonnet, with an octet that then has its reply in
the last six lines. The poem starts with a confident assertion that 'the
world is charged with the grandeur of God'. 'Grandeur' is well chosen
because it avoids the liturgical and obvious religious term 'glory', and
also is not quite 'sovereignty' or 'majesty'. It speaks of magnificence
and stylishness, and it alliterates comfortably with 'God'. 'Charged'
is also stunningly good. It is an early poetic use of the metaphor of
electricity (experiments in which were causing considerable excite-
ment at the time), and it expresses the existence of an unseen, mys-
terious force that seems to be inherent in the nature of things. The
second line speaks of how this force does sometimes, as in an epiph-
any, become briefly and gloriously visible, like in a lightning strike
or, indeed, as had been demonstrated in recent experiments using
gold foil. 'Shining from shook foil' uses alliteration to highlight the
shivery, intermittent nature of the glimpses of inherent glory.

The poet then shifts to a different metaphor, that of olive oil being
pressed out in a slow, steady way to produce something that also
speaks of God: oil that nourishes, provides light, and is the medium
for religious anointing. So we have contrasting images, the first sug-
gesting a proactive, powerful and quite dangerous force, the second
a life-giving and soothing substance that humans can handle and
which passively 'gathers to a greatness' precisely when it is 'Crushed'.

Notice what force the word 'Crushed' has, where it is placed alone at the beginning of a line. God's grandeur is seen through nature's lens in both his fiery creativity and in his acceptance of being crushed in the service of humanity. Hence the narrator's query about people's obliviousness to such a God, so manifest in all his works: 'Why do men then now not reck his rod?' Each word here, being a single syllable, requires emphasis. 'Reck' means to reckon, or pay heed to, and 'rod' implies God's authority.

The next line picks up the rhyme, with a threefold repetition of the word 'trod'; you can almost sense the endless generations of humans that have trodden the earth (and, it is implied, heedlessly trampled it). The next set of rhymes implies damage: 'seared ... bleared ... smeared'. There is a sense that the world has been scarred through the demands of human industry, but also that humans have not thereby benefited. We have 'bleared' our vision, and made things dirty that were not so before our interference. The sense of shame and disgust carries on with a new alliteration ('man's smudge ... man's smell'), emphasizing how we have set our mark on the landscape but in a way that spoils its beauty and hangs around like a toxic odour. This is not really deliberate, but is the consequence of losing our contact with the earth; the soil is bare now but our insensitive feet are not: 'nor can foot feel, being shod'. (Again, that blunt oppositional rhyme with 'God'.)

But at the start of the sestet a new direction is set, and the poem recovers the exultant tone of its confident beginning: in spite of human exploitation and indifference, 'nature is never spent;/ There lives the dearest freshness deep down things'. This is a beautiful assertion of the integrity of the natural world, and its capacity for endlessly returning to the freshness of the moment of creation, since the grandeur of the creator inhabits every particle of it like a charge. Pointing out that the pattern of day and night, sunset and new dawning are a constant cycle around the globe, the poem now builds towards the line that indeed recalls the moment of creation, when, as Genesis puts it, 'the Spirit of God was moving over the face of the waters', before things were brought into being (Genesis 1.2). Many have observed that this description recalls the brooding of a bird that is hatching new life (and of course the Holy Spirit is often depicted as a dove); and Hopkins' details of the 'warm breast' and 'ah! bright wings' give concreteness and intimacy to this image. It may also recall the cry of Jesus as he contemplates the city of Jerusalem where he will die, and which will itself soon be destroyed by the Romans: 'How often would I have gathered your children together as a hen gathers her brood under her wings, and you would not!' (Luke 13.34).

Of course, as we have seen, the Holy Spirit also plays a crucial part in the conception of Jesus, so here we have brought together the act of creation, the event of the Incarnation, and the memory of Jesus' death and the redemption of the world, in one extraordinary, short, celebratory poem. That world remains 'bent' and smudged by generations of the sins of humanity, but it is, deep down, still fresh and radiant with the unquenchable glory of God, made manifest to those with the eyes to see.

'The world is charged with the grandeur of God.' As you go through your day, try to look at the world through the lens of this poem.

Acknowledgements

The Collect for Advent Sunday is taken from the Book of Common Prayer, the rights in which are vested in the Crown. Extracts are reproduced by permission of the Crown's Patentee, Cambridge University Press.

W. H. Auden, 'Musée des Beaux Arts', in *Collected Poems*, Faber and Faber, 1976, copyright © 1940 by W. H. Auden, renewed. Reprinted by permission of Curtis Brown, Ltd.

Charles Causley, 'Innocent's Song', in *Collected Poems*, Macmillan, 1992, used by permission of David Higham Associates Ltd.

Gillian Clarke, 'Ode to Winter' and 'The Year's Midnight', in *Ice*, Carcanet Press, 2012, used by permission of Carcanet Press Ltd.

T. S. Eliot, 'Journey of the Magi', in *Collected Poems 1909–1962*, Faber and Faber Ltd, 1963, used by permission of Faber and Faber Ltd.

Ruth Fainlight, 'The Other', in *New and Collected Poems*, Bloodaxe Books, 2010, used by permission of Bloodaxe Books.

U. A. Fanthorpe, 'BC:AD', in *New and Collected Poems*, Enitharmon Press, 2010, copyright © R. V. Bailey.

Harry Gilonis, 'seasonal *ghazal*', in *The Twelve Poems of Christmas*, Vol. III, ed. Carol Ann Duffy, Candlestick, 2011, used by kind permission of the author.

Kerry Hardie, 'Autumn's Fall', used by kind permission of the author and The Gallery Press, Loughcrew, Oldcastle, County Meath, Ireland, from *Selected Poems* (2011).

Elizabeth Jennings, 'November Sonnet' and 'The Visitation', in *Collected Poems*, Carcanet Press, 2012, used by permission of David Higham Associates Ltd.

P. J. Kavanagh, 'Blackbird in Fulham', in *Collected Poems*, Carcanet Press, 1992, used by permission of Carcanet Press Ltd.

Acknowledgements

Jane Kenyon, 'The Bat' and 'Winter Solstice' from *Collected Poems*. Copyright © 2005 by The Estate of Jane Kenyon. Reprinted with the permission of The Permissions Company, Inc. on behalf of Graywolf Press, www.graywolfpress.org.

Philip Larkin, 'Church Going', in *The Complete Poems*, Faber and Faber Ltd, 2012, used by permission of Faber and Faber Ltd.

Denise Levertov, 'Agnus Dei', in *The Stream and the Sapphire*, New Directions, 1997, reproduced by permission of Pollinger Limited and New Directions.

Gwyneth Lewis, 'Annunciation', in *Chaotic Angels – Poems in English*, Bloodaxe Books, 2005, used by permission of Bloodaxe Books.

Edwin Muir, 'The Annunciation', in *Selected Poems*, Faber and Faber Ltd, 2008, used by permission of Faber and Faber Ltd.

Alan Payne, 'Darkness – *after Rilke*', used by kind permission of the author.

Sylvia Plath, 'Black Rook in Rainy Weather', in *Collected Poems*, Faber and Faber Ltd, 1981, used by permission of Faber and Faber Ltd.

Kathleen Raine, 'Northumbrian Sequence, 4' and 'Winter Paradise' by Kathleen Raine appear by permission of The Literary Estate of Kathleen Raine, copyright © 2000.

Vernon Scannell, 'Song for a Winter Birth', in *The Winter Man* (1973), reprinted in *Collected Poems 1950–1993*, Robson Books, 1993, used by permission of The Estate of Vernon Scannell.

R. S. Thomas, 'The Absence', in *Frequencies*, Macmillan, 1978, copyright © Kunjana Thomas.

Rowan Williams, 'In the Days of Caesar' (translation from the Welsh of Waldo Williams) and 'Advent Calendar', from *The Poems of Rowan Williams* (2002), reprinted by permission of the author and the publisher, The Perpetua Press.

Judith Wright, 'Woman to Child' in *A Human Pattern – Selected Poems*, ETT Imprint, Sydney, 2010, used by permission of ETT Imprint.

All biblical quotations are taken from the Revised Standard Version of the Bible, copyright © 1946, 1952, and 1971 the Division of Christian

Education of the National Council of the Churches of Christ in the United States of America. Used by permission. All rights reserved.

My grateful thanks are due to Dr Jill Robson and Nicky Woods, who commented on my draft. Any remaining errors or inaccuracies are of course my own.